Reproducible Activities

Brain Games

Mind-Stretching Classroom Activities

Grades 6-8

By
Ann Fisher

Cover Design by
Peggy Jackson

Published by Instructional Fair • TS Denison
an imprint of

About the Author

Ann Fisher, a former elementary teacher, is presently a freelance educational writer. She has many published books and magazine articles with several leading educational publishers. Ann graduated from Northern Michigan University. After spending time working with her husband Keith in a cross-community charity in Newcastle, Northern Ireland, and later working in the Republic of Ireland, Ann, her husband, and their children, Bryce and Betsy, now live in Mill Hall, Pennsylvania.

Credits
Author: Ann Fisher
Cover Design: Peggy Jackson
Project Director/Editor: Jerry Aten
Editors: Debra Olson Pressnall, Kathryn Wheeler, Sara Bierling
Page Design: Peggy Jackson
Page Production: Kruse Graphic Design, C.J. Designs

McGraw-Hill
Children's Publishing
A Division of The McGraw-Hill Companies

Published by Instructional Fair • TS Denison
An imprint of McGraw-Hill Children's Publishing

Send all inquiries to:
McGraw-Hill Children's Publishing
3195 Wilson Drive NW
Grand Rapids, Michigan 49544

Brain Games—grades 6-8
ISBN: 0-7424-0213-4

1 2 3 4 5 6 7 8 9 07 06 05 04 03 02

BRAIN GAMES is an exciting collection of fun and educationally sound classroom activities that will put your middle schoolers' brains to work. Whether you are looking for individual challenges for those students who always finish work early, games for small groups, or activities to engage the entire class, you are certain to find helpful activities. Many of the games labeled "Problem Solving" involve critical thinking skills that reach across the curriculum and are appropriate for advisory class periods or any other time. The games are arranged into 3 easy-to-use sections.

GAMES FOR INDIVIDUALS

The first section of this book is written for students who can work independently. This assortment includes practice in logic, number skills, word play, problem solving, following directions, and more. We suggest that you keep a folder of these reproducible activities in a place where students can access them in their free time. Answers to the Games for Individuals appear at the end of the section. You may want students to check their own work. If so, reproduce the answer pages and separate the keys by cutting along dotted lines. Keep these answers in a separate folder where students can access answers only with your permission.

PARTNER OR SMALL-GROUP GAMES

There is no better way to promote cooperation than to let a few students work through a game together. For some games, students will be competing against each other; in others, students will be working together toward a common objective. Again, we suggest that you keep a folder of reproducible games in a place where students can access them without your help. Some games require dice, toothpicks, and other supplies. Instructions and materials needed to play the game are included in the introduction on each page. A few of the games require answer keys which appear at the end of this section. Follow the directions in the previous paragraph regarding answer keys.

ENTIRE-CLASS GAMES

Perfect for a Friday afternoon or the last day before vacation, here you will find games to challenge everyone at once. These are teacher-directed activities, and answers (when needed) appear with each game. Many require the use of an overhead projector. For others, the chalkboard or pencil and paper are enough. Several different multipurpose game formats are also suggested. You will be able to adapt almost any material to some of these formats. For other games, exact questions are included so that you need to do very little preparation.

No matter how many of your students are ready and willing to play educational games, you will be well prepared with the activities included in this book!

Table of Contents

Games for Individuals

Partner Games

Entire-Class Games

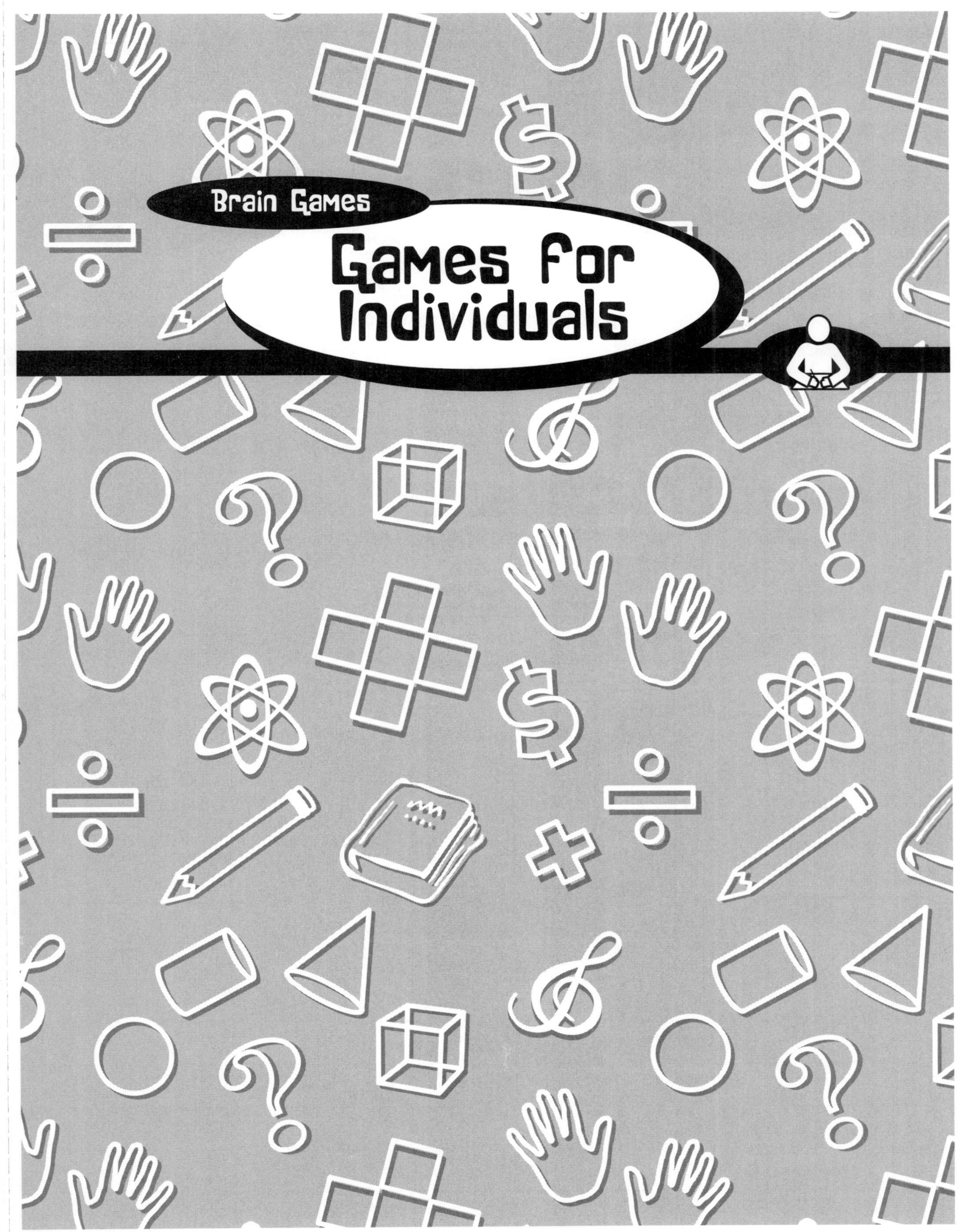
Brain Games
Games for Individuals

Name ______________________ Date ______________

Can you beat this baffler by filling the blanks below with acceptable words? The object of this game is to spell as many words as possible, moving around among letter boxes that are next to each other. Here are the rules for this page:

1. Spell only 4-letter words.
2. Do not use proper nouns.
3. Start your word on any letter, and move to any other letter that touches it vertically, horizontally, or diagonally.
4. You may not come back to a letter you have already used in the same word.

Allow yourself 15 minutes for this game. After time has run out, you may check your list for repeated words or words that are not correct.

Examples that work: dirt, meow

Examples that don't work: tide, plop

P	L	E	C
W	O	D	I
E	T	R	N
M	U	G	A

Score your work this way:

20 words A+
16–19 words A
13–15 words A
10–12 words B+
8–9 words B
6–7 words B
5 words or less TRY AGAIN!

______	______	______	______
______	______	______	______
______	______	______	______
______	______	______	______
______	______	______	______
______	______	______	______

Name ______________________ Date ______________

If you successfully completed the previous page, perhaps you will find this one to be more of a challenge. The object of this game again is to spell as many words as possible, moving around among letter boxes that are next to each other. Here are the rules:

1. Spell only 5-letter words.
2. Do not use proper nouns, plurals, or the -s form of verbs (like eats).
3. Start your word on any letter, and move to any other letter that touches it vertically, horizontally, or diagonally.
4. You may not come back to a letter you have already used in the same word.

Allow yourself 20 minutes for this game. Write as many 5-letter words as possible. After time has run out, you may check your list for repeated words or words that are not correct.

Example that works: reach

Example that doesn't work: brain

y	l	f	e	c
e	d	r	t	h
m	a	s	n	a
i	c	e	b	k
l	h	r	i	n

Score your work this way:
16 words A+
14–15 words A
12–13 words A
10–11 words B+
8–9 words B
6–7 words B
5 words or less TRY AGAIN!

______________ ______________ ______________ ______________

______________ ______________ ______________ ______________

______________ ______________ ______________ ______________

______________ ______________ ______________ ______________

______________ ______________ ______________ ______________

______________ ______________ ______________ ______________

How many times can you score 50 during the next 15 minutes? Choose one number from each column so that the sum of the 3 numbers is 50. Draw lines between the numbers as you use them. One example is shown for you.

If you can find 6 or more combinations in the next 15 minutes, you have done very well. If you want to take more time, try to find the solution that uses all the numbers and scores 50 a total of 12 times. If you can find this solution, you are truly remarkable!

25	18	22
13	6	20
9	30	15
11	21	21
12	12	25
15	19	24
19	17	2
14	29	13
7	15	8
18	16	20
16	17	28
10	23	10

Name ______________________________ Date ______________

Here is a puzzle that will test your skills in logic. See how quickly you can solve it. Two girls, Amber and Brittany, and two boys, Casey and Dirk, all live in different states of the U.S.A. Read the clues to find out the home state of each person. You will need a map of the United States and the list of the 50 states shown here.

Alabama Alaska Arizona Arkansas California Colorado Connecticut Delaware Florida Georgia Hawaii Idaho Illinois Indiana Iowa Kansas Kentucky Louisiana Maine Maryland Massachusetts Michigan Minnesota Mississippi Missouri Montana Nebraska Nevada New Hampshire New Jersey New Mexico New York North Carolina North Dakota Ohio Oklahoma Oregon Pennsylvania Rhode Island South Carolina South Dakota Tennessee Texas Utah Vermont Virginia Washington West Virginia Wisconsin Wyoming

1. Three people live in the continental United States; one does not.
2. No one lives in a state that begins with **M**.
3. Casey and Dirk live west of the Mississippi River.
4. One of the girls lives in a state which has a coastline on both the Atlantic Ocean and the Gulf of Mexico.
5. The other girl (the one not mentioned in Clue 4) lives in a state that has more than one set of double letters in its name.
6. Dirk lives in a state with a 2-word name.
7. Casey and Amber both live in states with names that end in **a**.
8. Dirk lives in a state that does not border another country.

Write your answers here:

Amber lives in________________. Brittany lives in________________.

Casey lives in________________. Dirk lives in________________.

Name ______________________ Date ______________

Here are 3 little games to test your abilities in divergent thinking. You do not need skills in computation, making tables, or trial-and-error. Instead, you need to approach each of these in a creative manner. Ask yourself how you can modify, rearrange, or adapt the existing situation in a new manner. Good Luck!

1. Draw 4 straight lines that pass through all the points without lifting your pencil or retracing your path.

•   •   •

•   •   •

•   •   •

2. Move 1 coin so that you have 4 coins in each row.

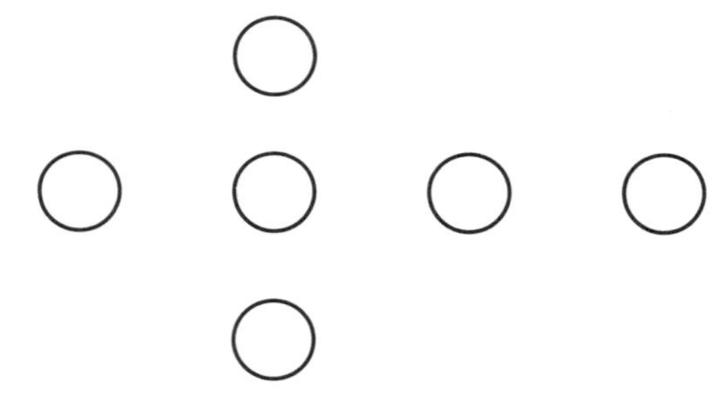

3. Arrange 9 toothpicks to create 3 triangles as shown. Then move 3 toothpicks to make 5 triangles.

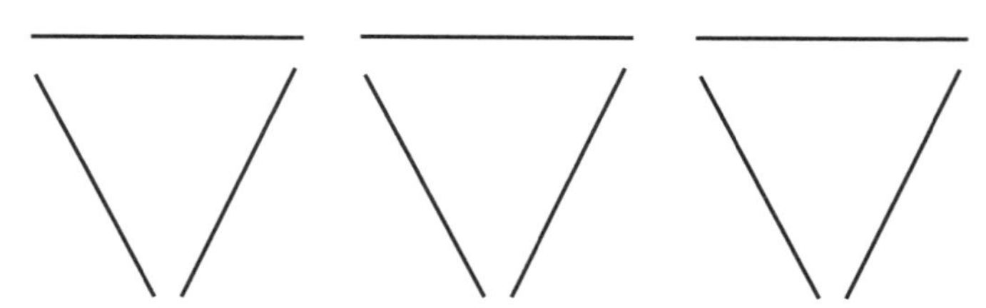

Name ______________________ Date ____________

Language Arts

Tricky Treats

Sweet Tooth Jones is opening a new candy store. He wants his shop to be very organized, and he wants to arrange the candies named here into the categories listed below.

Cut out the markers from the side of this page, and decide how they can be arranged into the 3 groups listed here. Move them around until you find a solution in which every treat has a place. Some treats appear to fit in more than 1 place, but you need a solution where every treat has a place.

1. Treats with double consonants:

__________ __________

__________ __________

2. Treats with 8 letters:

__________ __________

__________ __________

3. Treats with 3 syllables:

__________ __________

__________ __________

- bubble gum
- candy bar
- candy corn
- gumdrops
- taffy apple
- lollipop
- homemade fudge
- jellybeans
- rock candy
- licorice
- marshmallow chicks
- lemon drops

Name ______________________ Date ______________

Take a tour across America as you unscramble these anagrams! The letters in each phrase below do not make much sense, but they can be rearranged to spell the name of one of our 50 states. How many can you solve? There is no time limit, so take as long as you need. When you are finished, score your work as shown in the box.

Example: vane ad Nevada

10 or more: Super genius!
7–9: Terrific!
5–6: Very good!

1. rat on oil ranch ______________________
2. It is grave win ______________________
3. saw nothing ______________________
4. many lard ______________________
5. O, or a clod ______________________
6. bank eras ______________________
7. acing him ______________________
8. Wade, Earl! ______________________
9. her sane whimp ______________________
10. foil in a car ______________________
11. TV or men ______________________
12. I, lan, a soul ______________________

Name ______________________________ Date ____________________

Now that you have toured some states of the U.S, it is time to visit some cities. Once again, the phrases are not very meaningful, but the letters in each phrase can be rearranged to spell the name of a major U.S. city. How many can you solve? There is no time limit, so take as long as you need. When you are finished, score your work as shown in the box.

Example: haven sill Nashville

10 or more: Super genius!
7–9: Terrific!
5–6: Very good!

1. gal heir ______________________
2. Luke, we aim ______________________
3. hip oxen ______________________
4. plant rod ______________________
5. help a hip dial ______________________
6. scorn a team ______________________
7. red to it ______________________
8. spoil in name ______________________
9. the ol' cart ______________________
10. oven priced ______________________
11. I'm on sad ______________________
12. Shout on! ______________________

Name ______________________ Date ______________

Math

Toothpick Tricks

Grab a handful of toothpicks and see if you can figure out these tricks. Make a sketch of the solutions you find, then check them with your teacher's answers.

1. Arrange 17 toothpicks as shown here to form 6 squares. Remove 5 toothpicks and leave just 3 squares.

Your solution:

2. Arrange 12 toothpicks as shown to form 1 large square and 4 smaller squares. Rearrange or remove toothpicks as directed, always starting with this arrangement:

Your solutions:

a)

b)

c)

d)

a) Move 3 toothpicks to new places and form just 3 squares.

b) Move 2 toothpicks and make 7 squares.

c) Move 4 toothpicks and leave 3 squares.

d) Move 4 toothpicks and make 10 squares.

Name ______________________________ Date ________________

Toothpick Tricks

(Continued)

3. Arrange 24 toothpicks as shown to form 9 small squares and several larger squares. Rearrange or remove toothpicks as directed, always starting with this arrangement:

a) Remove 6 toothpicks and leave 3 squares.
b) Remove 8 toothpicks and leave just 2 squares.
c) Remove 8 toothpicks and leave 3 squares.

Your solutions:
a)

b)

c)

4. Use 8 toothpicks to form 2 squares and 4 triangles.

5. Lay 6 toothpicks on your desk, parallel to each other, as shown. Add 5 more toothpicks, without rearranging the first 6, to make 9. (Note: This is possible! Check your teacher's solution if you can't find one.)

6. Create 3 squares with 12 toothpicks as shown. Take away any 2 toothpicks and rearrange the others to leave 2.

Name ______________________ Date ______________

Here is a puzzle that should not take 4 months to complete, but you WILL be using the names of 4 months of the year! Keep the months in the same order as they appear below (and on the calendar). Then create as many 4-letter words as possible by using 1 letter at a time from each month. For example, use the **S** in September, the **T** in October, the **E** in November, and the **M** in December to spell STEM.

Try to write several more words in this same manner. Score your work as shown in the box.

SEPTEMBER

OCTOBER

NOVEMBER

DECEMBER

12 or more words: Superior
9–11 words: Excellent
6–8 words: Good
5 or less: Keep working

Words created:

______	______	______
______	______	______
______	______	______
______	______	______
______	______	______
______	______	______
______	______	______

Name ______________________________ Date ______________

How much help do you need to complete this chart? First, see how many boxes you can fill working by yourself. Supply a word for each category beginning with letters H, E, L, and P. For instance, you might write *horse* for the first box because it is a mammal beginning with H. Give yourself 5 points for each space you fill. Then use a reference book to help you fill in the rest of the spaces. Give yourself 2 points for every space you fill in this way. Find your total score when you've completed the entire chart. Remember: 100 points equals a perfect score.

	H	E	L	P
mammals				
European cities				
famous authors (last name)				
birds				
U.S. Presidents (last name)				

Name ______________________ Date ______________

If you are "brainy" about birds, then hopefully you can decode these 12 types of birds. Here is how: Think of a word to fit each clue, and then use a portion of those letters to spell a type of bird.

Example: $\frac{3}{5}$ of a thief + $\frac{1}{4}$ of moderately hot
To solve: $\frac{3}{5}$ of *crook* + $\frac{1}{4}$ of *warm* = cro + w = crow

Note: Fractions are given in lowest terms. For instance, a clue that calls for half of a word might actually use 2 letters of a 4-letter word or 3 letters of a 6-letter word, etc.

1. $\frac{2}{3}$ of a male sheep + $\frac{3}{5}$ of snake's poison = ______________________
2. $\frac{2}{3}$ of what a chicken lays + $\frac{1}{2}$ of to go back = ______________________
3. $\frac{2}{5}$ of a marsh + $\frac{2}{7}$ of very old = ______________________
4. $\frac{1}{2}$ of a chair occupied by a king + $\frac{3}{5}$ of one who escorts people to their seats in a theater = ______________________
5. $\frac{3}{5}$ of a manlike mechanical device + $\frac{2}{5}$ of an alphabetical list of subjects in the back of a book = ______________________
6. $\frac{3}{5}$ of emerald + $\frac{2}{5}$ of a sandy shore = ______________________
7. $\frac{3}{5}$ of the last + $\frac{2}{5}$ of inexpensive = ______________________
8. $\frac{1}{2}$ of every + $\frac{3}{4}$ of joy = ______________________
9. $\frac{3}{4}$ of a large cove + $\frac{1}{4}$ of molten rock from a volcano = ______________________
10. $\frac{4}{5}$ of strong winds with rain or snow + $\frac{1}{3}$ of a lock opener = ______________________
11. $\frac{1}{3}$ of frozen water + $\frac{1}{2}$ to cut into 2 parts = ______________________
12. $\frac{1}{2}$ of a shaped mass of bread + $\frac{1}{2}$ of one time only = ______________________

Consider yourself a real "birdbrain" if you were able to solve at least 10 of these!

Name ______________________________ Date ______________

Phoney Numbers

Dial up some fun with this challenge! Look at the phone keypad on the right. Notice that on the telephone, each number can represent different letters. For example, a 3 can represent a D, E, or F.

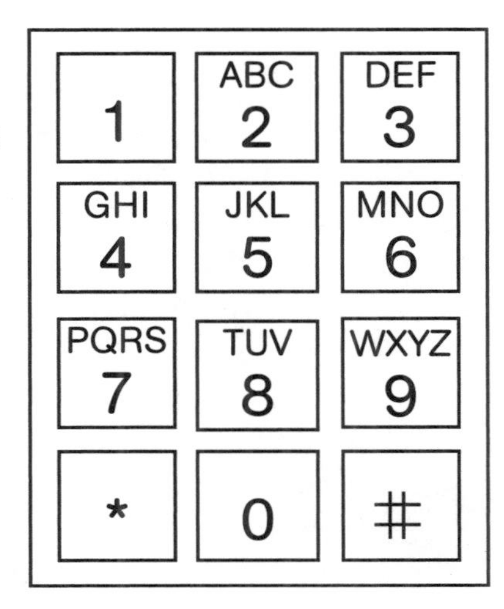

Imagine that a seaside resort wants to use a phone number that is easy to remember. The owner arranges with the phone company to use the number 229-8439. These numbers spell the phrase BAY-VIEW.

Now try to determine what word or phrase is intended by each of the companies listed below. Write your final answer in each blank.

1. Freddy's Fresh Vegetables: 732-7637 ______________________
2. Melodic Musical Instruments: 539-6683 ______________________
3. Polly's Premium Plumbing Service: 349-5325 ______________________
4. Top-Notch Television Reporters: 244-6397 ______________________
5. Connie's Personal Portable Computers: 527-8677 ______________________
6. Fast Financial Freedom Corporation: 438-2274 ______________________
7. Boise's Best Barber: 288-4247 ______________________
8. Deidre's Dieting Center: 328-5377 ______________________
9. Parkview's Public Playground: 386-8463 ______________________
10. Waldo's Workout Wonder Gym: 348-6377 ______________________

Name ______________________ Date ______________

On these 2 pages you will find some great "Sum Puzzlers." You simply need to arrange the specified numbers according to directions so that certain rows of numbers have the same total. To help you try many different solutions without the frustration of erasing, cut out numbered markers from scrap paper. Then move them around from place to place. Be sure to read the directions for each puzzler very carefully, because each one is a little different from the others. When you find a solution that works, write it into the puzzle with your pencil.

1. Place each of the numerals 1, 2, 3, 4, and 5 in the circles of the "T" so that the sum of the 3 numbers in each direction is the same. Try to find several different ways to do this.

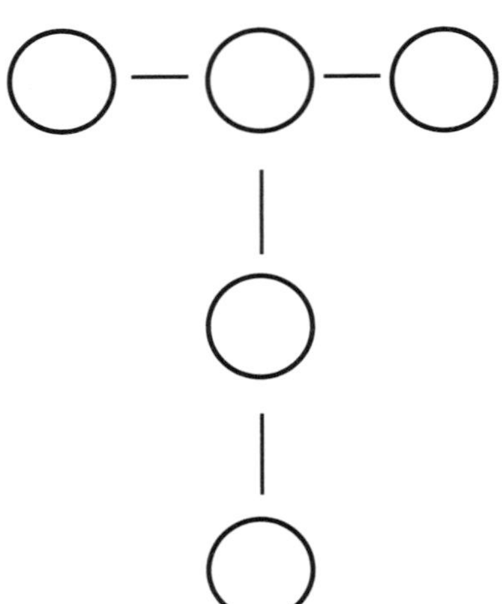

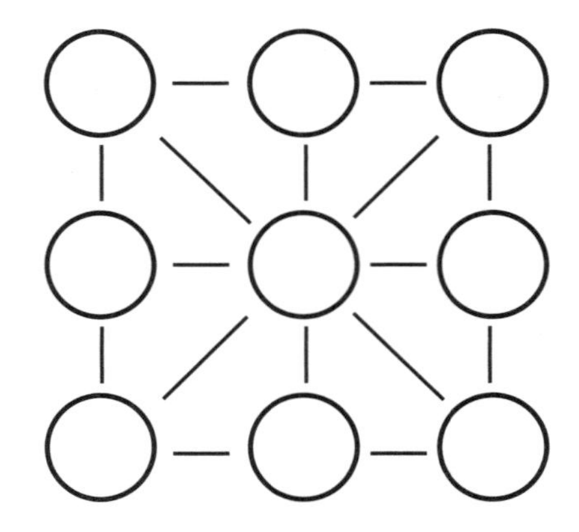

2. Arrange the numbers from 5 to 13 in the circles so that the sum of each row, column, and diagonal is 27.

Name ______________________ Date ______________

3. Complete this diamond by arranging the numerals from 10 to 18 in the circles so that the sum of each line of circles is 42.

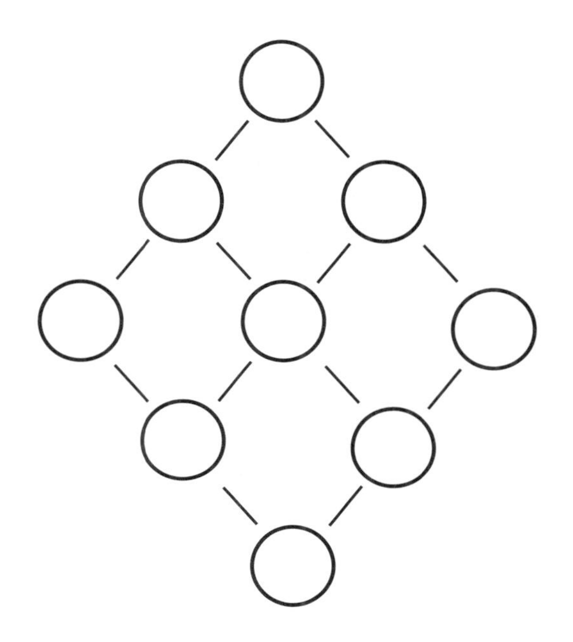

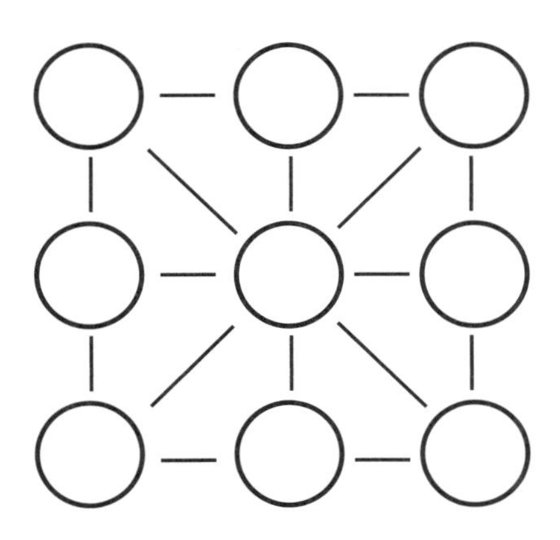

4. Arrange the even numbers from 2 to 18 in the circles so that each row, column, and diagonal has the same sum. Try to figure out what the best sum might be. If you have trouble with that, ask your teacher to check the answer key for some help.

Name ______________________________ Date ______________

Do you have a-MAZE-ing number skills? Here is your chance to find out.

A. First start on the left-hand side of the maze at the arrow. With your pencil, continue drawing a path all the way through the maze to the right-hand edge of the maze so that the numbers on each side of your line are multiples of 3 (0, 3, 6, 9, etc.).

B. For your next path, use a different colored pencil if possible. Start at the arrow at the top of the maze. Draw a line through the entire maze so that the sum of the numbers on either side of your line is a prime number. (Remember, a prime number is one that can only be divided evenly by 1 and itself.) At the beginning of this line you can see 5 and 6, and you know that 5 + 6 = 11. Eleven is a prime number.

C. Finally, find the 3 x 3 arrangement of numbers in the maze with the highest total. Outline it with your pencil.

10	20	3	5 ↓	6	3	12	18	2	10	16	1
15	2	27	7	1	1	3	28	15	19	13	11
31	17	4	11	2	3	9	2	1	9	2	8
11	30	9	21	8	4	4	19	26	2	14	13
33	8	12	34	29	9	32	0	11	6	16	17
10	4	10	12	30	3	27	6	7	1	20	15
18	9	3	9	24	15	6	3	0	3	19	11
→ 6	33	36	7	3	14	5	4	18	9	6	5
5	1	14	16	5	18	13	3	1	24	3	4
7	6	11	1	5	2	21	14	0	12	36	7
23	39	9	35	8	1	10	9	2	18	6	42
12	4	13	7	18	42	2	1	4	5	9	30
15	41	36	17	15	25	16	21	3	10	19	7
6	22	16	2	40	4	7	2	12	18	6	38
14	15	13	24	3	9	8	17	4	37	1	20

Name ______________________ Date ______________

Plan the Plots

Farmer Brown passed away and left his 4 sons his house and a piece of ground on which grew 8 fruit trees. The farmer's will stated that the house was to be shared by all the sons, but that each son was to have his own plot of ground. Each plot was to be of the same size and shape as the others, and each was to contain 2 trees. The will also directed that each son's ground should be situated so that he could step from his own plot into the yard of the house without setting foot on the land of his brothers.

If the plot of ground was shaped as shown here, with "H" representing the piece of land on which the house was built, how can the land be divided into 4 equal plots according to the terms of the will? Draw in your final answer.

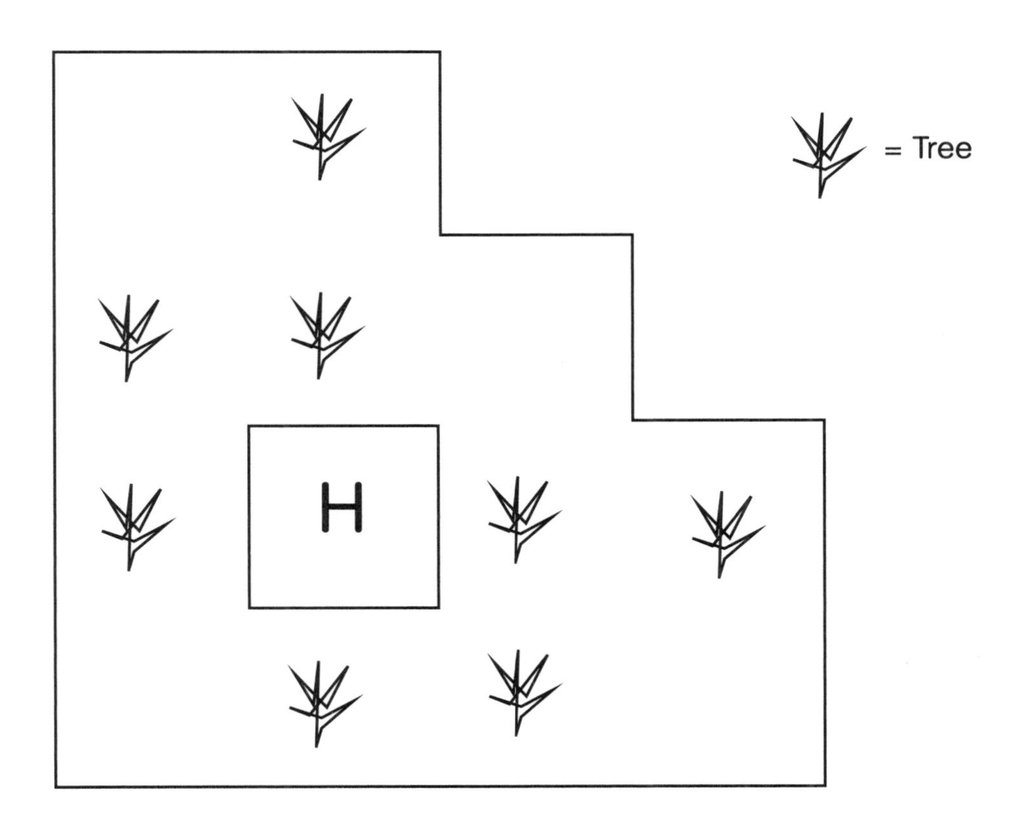

Name ______________________________ Date ______________

How quickly can you pick your brain (and your family tree) to find the answers to the questions below? For example, who is your father's father's son? It could be either *your dad* or *your uncle*. Think carefully as you match each description to the correct relative. You will need to use 1 answer twice. While there may be more than 1 answer for some items, pick from the choices given here. Assume that all married relatives are in their first marriage.

1. Your aunt's mother ________
2. Your aunt's mother's father's wife ________
3. Your father's uncle ________
4. Your uncle's father ________
5. Your father's uncle's brother's sister ________
6. Your brother's son's sister ________
7. Your sister's son's brother's father ________
8. Your brother's wife's father-in-law ________
9. Your sister-in-law's father-in-law's grandson ________
10. Your father's father's daughter's daughter ________
11. Your mother's mother-in-law ________
12. Your sister's husband's mother-in-law ________

A. your great-aunt
B. your great-uncle
C. your mother
D. your grandmother
E. your great-grandmother
F. your father
G. your grandfather
H. your brother-in-law
I. your cousin
J. your niece
K. your nephew

Name ______________________ Date ______________

Relative Riddles

Here is a chance for you to rattle your brain as you work through these riddles about family relatives. Think about the fathers, grandfathers, mothers, grandmothers, sisters, and brothers in your own family as you work. It may be helpful for you to draw sketches of possible family trees in order to answer some of the questions.

1. In a family where each son has twice as many sisters as he has brothers, and each daughter has the same number of brothers as sisters, how many boys are there and how many girls are there?

2. In your state, is a man allowed to marry his widow's sister?

3. Two room mothers had just met and were getting acquainted. Mrs. Jones said, "I have 6 daughters and each of my daughters has a brother." Mrs. Smith replied, "I don't see how with 12 children you could have time and energy to be a room mother, too." But Mrs. Jones answered, "I do not have 12, I only have 7 children." How can this be true?

4. Two fathers and two sons went hunting. They shot 3 ducks and divided them equally among themselves. They did this without shooting any more ducks or cutting any of the ducks. How was this possible?

5. Several cousins are playing together at a family picnic. It is little Ryan's birthday and he has just received a bag of marbles which he would like to share with at least some of his cousins. Ryan discovers that if he divides his new marbles into groups of 3, he has 1 extra. If he arranges them in groups of 4, he has 2 extras. If he divides them in groups of 5, he has 3 marbles left over. If he arranges them in groups of 6, he has 4 left. How many marbles were given to Ryan?

6. Molly is the only girl in the Wilson family and the eldest of her parents' 7 children. The children's ages run in 4-year steps, with Molly being 4 times as old as Sammy, the "baby" of the family. How old is Sammy?

7. If a family has 3 children, what is the likelihood that the 3 will be either all girls or all boys?

Name ______________________ Date ______________

Ornamental Spelling

These Christmas ornaments can be arranged to spell 6 holiday words of 6 letters each. To find the words, imagine sliding the ornaments along their strings so that the letters are lined up vertically. For example, using letters on the top 3 strings, you could spell the word *sun* going down. Note that while ornaments can be slid, they cannot be moved out of their current order on the strings. Also note that there are 3 extra ornaments in every line. Write the 6 words that you find on the back of this page.

Name ______________________ Date ______________

Money Matters

Lola and Leroy know that money matters because they own their own shoe store and must sell a lot of shoes in order to pay their bills. But they are not so good at managing their money. See if you can solve each of these money problems.

1. Lola sold a pair of shoes for $8 and received a $20 bill. She could not make change for the customer from her cash register, so she went to the convenience store next door and had the $20 bill changed for smaller bills. She went back to her customer and gave him $12 in change. When the convenience store owner did his banking, he learned that Lola's $20 bill was counterfeit. He went back to Lola and asked her to reimburse him for the fake bill. How much did Lola lose on this transaction?

2. A young child comes into the store and asks Lola to exchange his dollar bill for 50 coins so that he can have lots of change for vending machines. She can think of only one way to do this, but Leroy says there are 2 ways. Who is correct?

3. Leroy ran the store on Monday. He said to Lola at the end of the day, "The day's income was $70 plus half a day's earnings." On Tuesday, Lola ran the store. At the end of the day she said to Leroy, "Tuesday's income was one and one-half times Monday's income." How much did Lola take in on Tuesday? What was the total 2-day income for their store?

4. Leroy hired Sal to stock the shelves with many brand-new pairs of shoes. They agreed Sal would be paid 25¢ for each pair of shoes he shelved properly. When Sal was finished Leroy asked, "How many new pairs did you shelve?" Sal replied, "I walked to the back of the store and counted 50 pairs on my right. Then I turned around and counted 50 on my left." How much should Leroy pay to Sal?

5. Lola's uncle passed away and left $20,000 in his will, to be divided equally among his 2 nieces and 3 nephews. The 3 nephews all decided among themselves, however, to give half of their shares to be divided equally between the nieces. How much did Lola receive?

6. Not to be outdone by Lola, Leroy claims that he, too, recently received an inheritance. His was, he said, a rare coin from his great-grandfather's coin collection, with the date 650 B.C. How did Lola know that either his story or the coin was a fake?

Name ______________________ Date ____________

Parallel Problems

Here's a game to put your brain into high gear! You are not competing against anyone or any time limit. You just need to see if you can meet this challenge. Place the numbers from 1 to 12 in the diagram so that the sum of the corners of each parallelogram is 25. Cut out the markers at the bottom of the page. This will allow you to try many different solutions. When you have found an answer that works, remove the markers and write each number in the diagram.

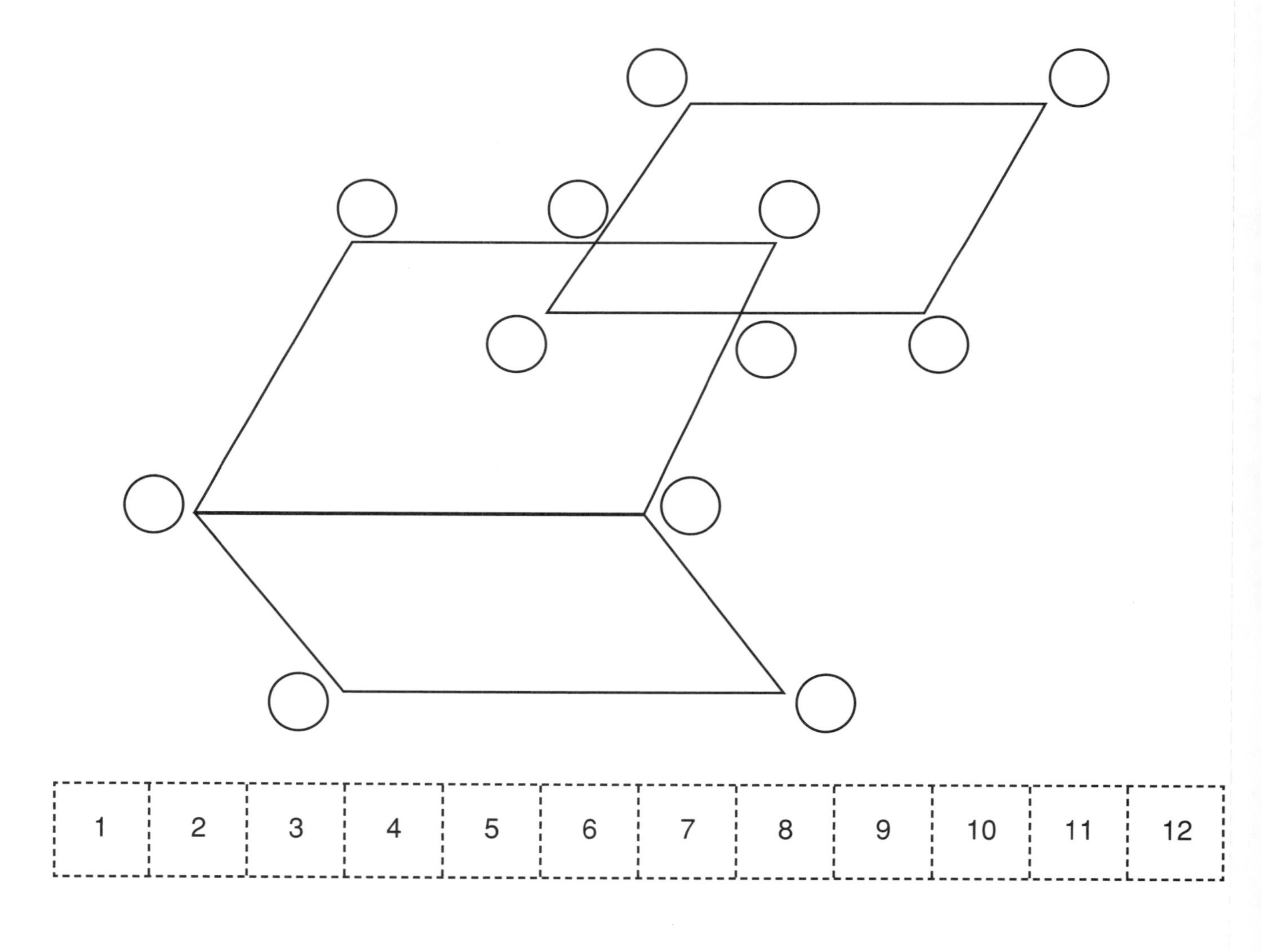

Name ______________________ Date ____________

Beware of the trouble that may be lurking inside your freezer! If you were to find this package of frozen meatballs, hopefully you would think twice before cooking and eating the contents. You will find several errors on the carton if you read it carefully. List each one that you find in the blanks below. You should find at least 10 errors.

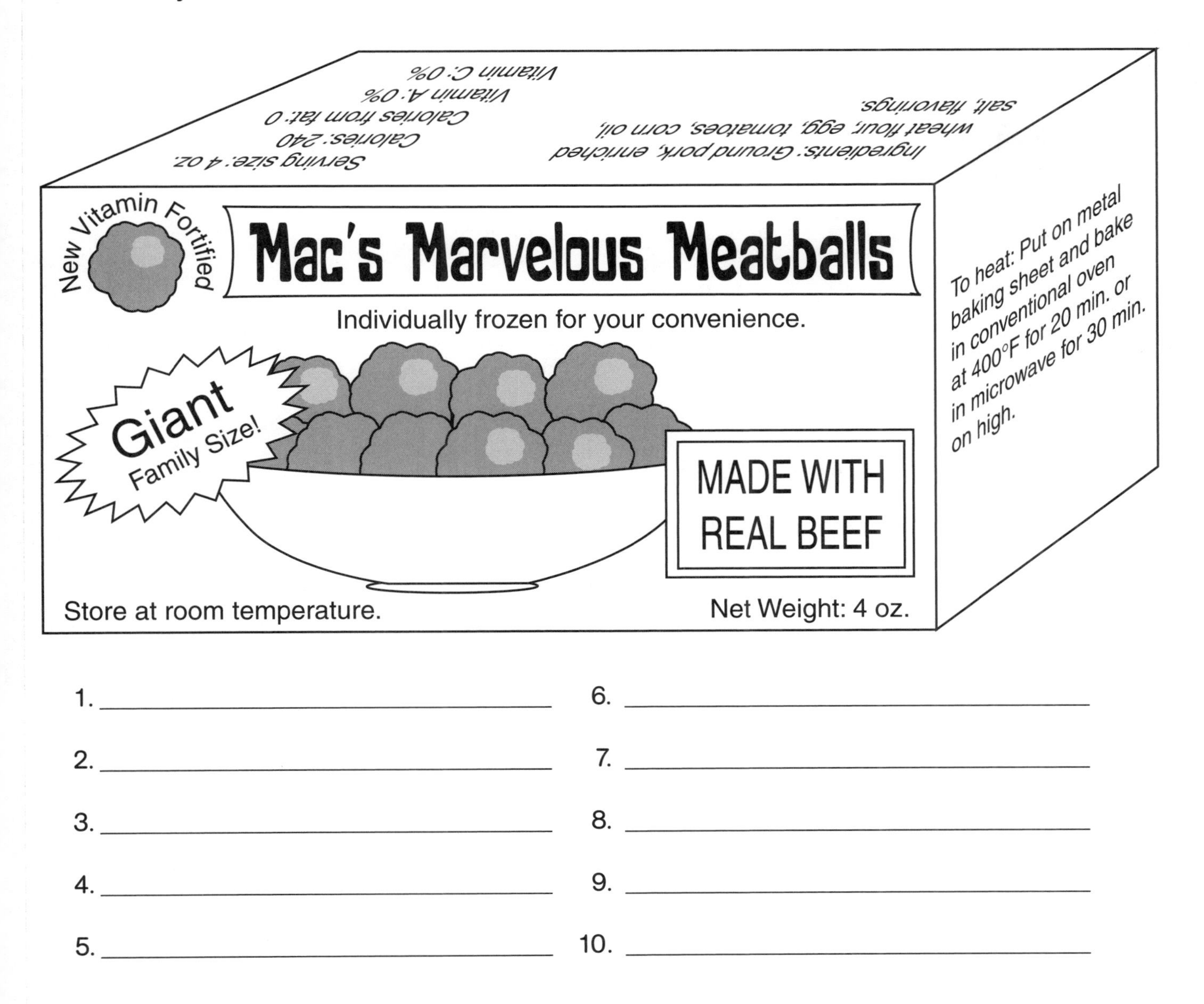

1. ______________________
2. ______________________
3. ______________________
4. ______________________
5. ______________________
6. ______________________
7. ______________________
8. ______________________
9. ______________________
10. ______________________

Name ______________________ Date ______________

A. Do you know the real size of many common objects? You are about to find out! First, which circle here is about the size of a quarter?

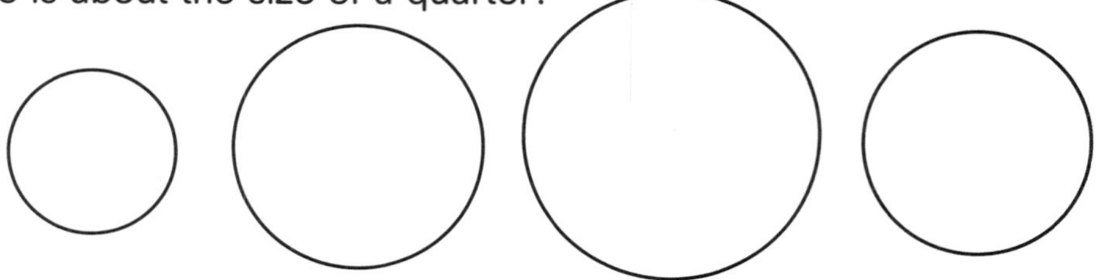

B. On the back of this page and on scrap paper, try to draw the right size for each item mentioned. Then check your answers against the real objects. You may be surprised!

1. A rectangle the size of a regular stick of chewing gum
2. A rectangle the size of a one-dollar bill
3. A line showing the height of a 12-ounce can of soda
4. A square the size of a computer floppy disk
5. A circle the size of a music CD
6. A line showing the length of an unsharpened No. 2 pencil
7. A rectangle the size of cassette tape
8. A square the size of a button on regular cordless phone
9. A line showing the length of an average car key

C. Now, rate your "sizing" skills. Choose one:
   1. I am nearly perfect!
   2. I was close on many of the objects.
   3. I was close on some of the objects.
   4. I completely misjudged every item!

If you are like most people, you will find yourself in either the second or third category.

Name ______________________ Date ______________

Can you crack this code? If you can, you will uncover 12 different parts or organs of the human body. Each coded letter represents a different letter of the alphabet. The same code works for the entire page. Hint: G = R

A	=	
B	=	
C	=	
D	=	
E	=	
F	=	
G	=	R
H	=	
I	=	
J	=	
K	=	
L	=	
M	=	
O	=	
P	=	
R	=	
S	=	
T	=	
U	=	
W	=	

1. W M U G F ______________
2. M I M ______________
3. K G U B C ______________
4. A J C O ______________
5. A B D M G ______________
6. E F H P U R W ______________
7. M U G ______________
8. F H C O J M ______________
9. S B L C M I ______________
10. K A U L L M G ______________
11. B C F M E F B C M ______________
12. T U C R G M U E ______________

Name ______________________ Date ____________

A Vexing Vine

Take a climb up this vine and see if you can find the word hidden on each leaf. Here is how: Start on the bottom leaf. Choose 1 letter from that word and push it up to the next leaf, leaving a familiar word at the bottom. Then choose 1 letter in the second leaf to push up to the third, leaving another common word behind in the second leaf. For example, push up the **p** in *spoil* to leave *soil* in the bottom leaf. All the words will share a common theme.

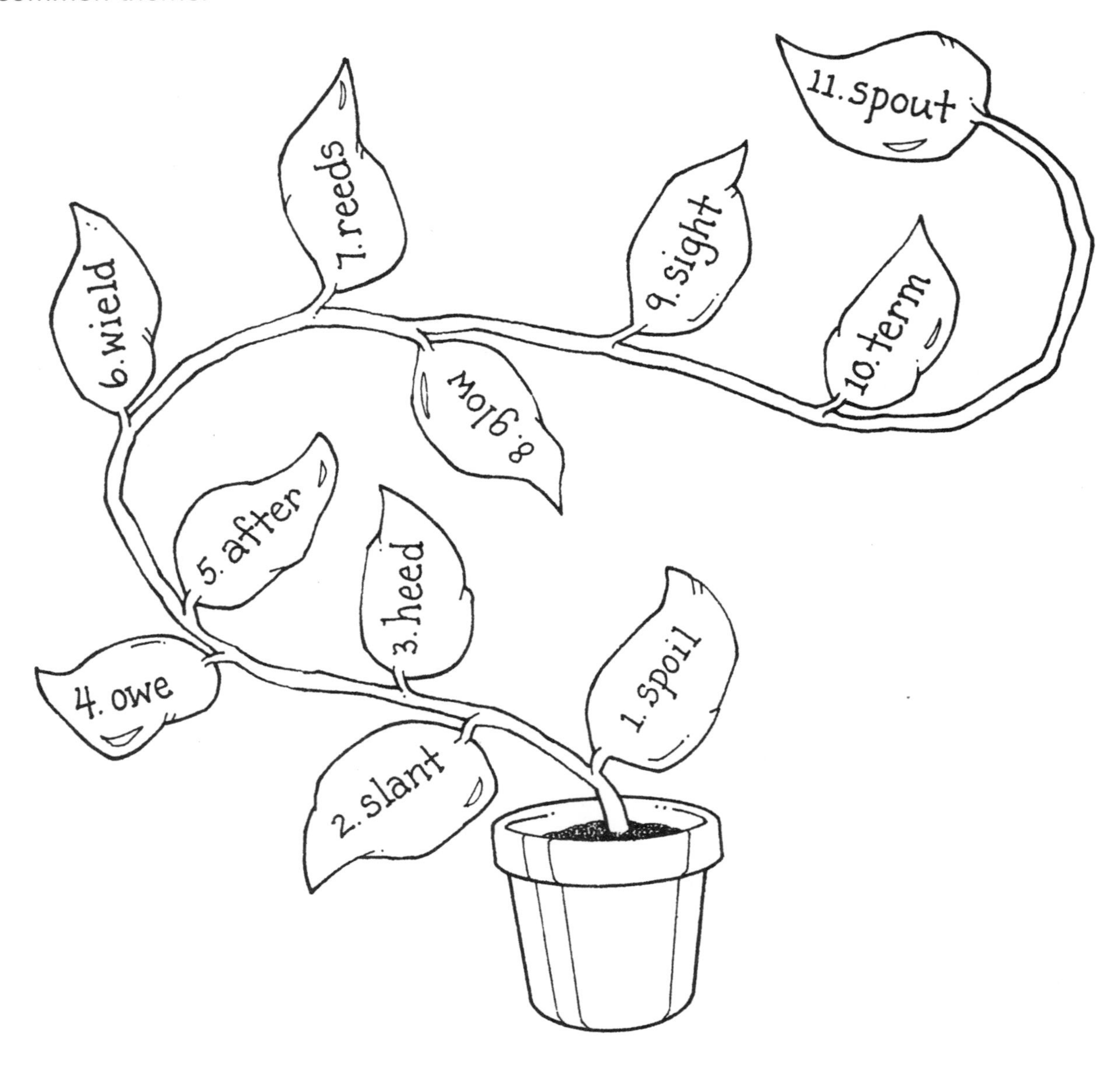

Name ______________________ Date ______________

What animal comes from the clouds? To find out, read the directions below. Be sure to carefully follow each instruction. When you cross out a number, also cross out the letter below it.

1	2	3	4	5	6	7	8	9	10	11	12	13	14	15
P	G	M	W	A	S	L	O	D	B	R	J	A	T	O

16	17	18	19	20	21	22	23	24	25	26	27	28	29	30
Q	U	E	N	F	L	Y	C	H	B	T	Z	U	D	S

1. Read all the directions before doing anything.
2. Cross out the number that is the same as your age.
3. Cross out all prime numbers.
4. Cross out all Ts.
5. Cross out all multiples of 5.
6. Cross out all multiples of 8.
7. Cross out all even numbers between 1 and 11.
8. Cross out all numbers less than 10 that divide evenly into 45.
9. Cross out all letters that come after **U** in the alphabet.
10. Cross out all multiples of 7 greater than 15.
11. Substitute each remaining letter with the one that comes before it in the alphabet.
12. Reverse the remaining letters.
13. Write the final letters here: ___ ___ ___ ___ , ___ ___ ___ ___ !
14. Do not do any of instructions numbered 2, 5, 7 and 12.

Name ______________________ Date ______________

Take a trip down memory lane as you study all the items on these toy store shelves. Remember how fun a new puzzle, book, doll, or truck was when you were young? Look at the toys very carefully for 1 minute. Then turn this page over and try to answer the questions on the next page.

Name ______________________________ Date ______________

After you have studied the picture from the toy store for 1 minute, turn that page over and answer these questions:

1. What is the name of the toy store?____________________
2. How many shelves are in the picture?____________________
3. What toy is right beside the rag doll?____________________
4. On which shelf are the books?____________________
5. How many books are on the shelf?____________________
6. Write the titles of 2 books:____________________
7. What game is under the books?____________________
8. What is the price of the teddy bear?____________________
9. What 2 toys cost less than a dollar?____________________
10. What toy is directly under the sign?____________________
11. What toy is on sale?____________________
12. On what shelf is the box of art supplies?____________________
13. What 2 toys are meant to be blown through to make noise?____________________
14. How many blocks are on the top shelf?____________________
15. What game is next to the teddy bear?____________________

When you have done your best in answering these questions, turn over the picture and check your answers. How good were your toy store memories?

Name ______________________ Date ______________

Places, Please!

Here are 2 fun number games that do NOT involve addition. See how quickly you can solve each one!

1. Use the numerals 1–8 so that no two connected circles contain successive numerals. For example, if you placed the 1 in the top center circle, you could not put the 2 in any of the 3 circles in the next row. To solve the puzzle, there will be only 1 instance where 2 numbers in a row are successive numerals.

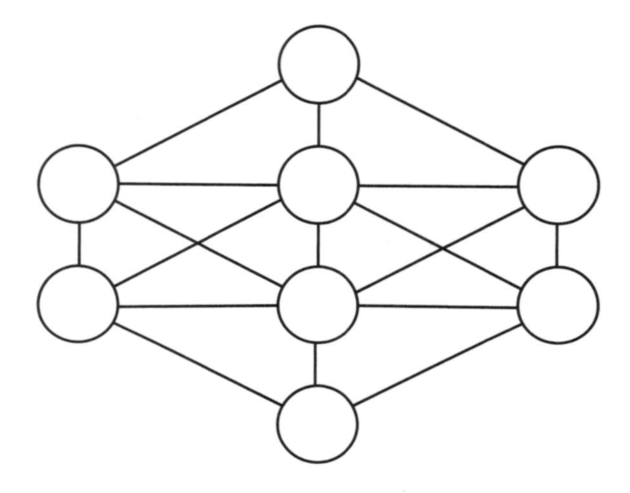

2. Now try to find what number is missing in this diagram. Can you figure it out?

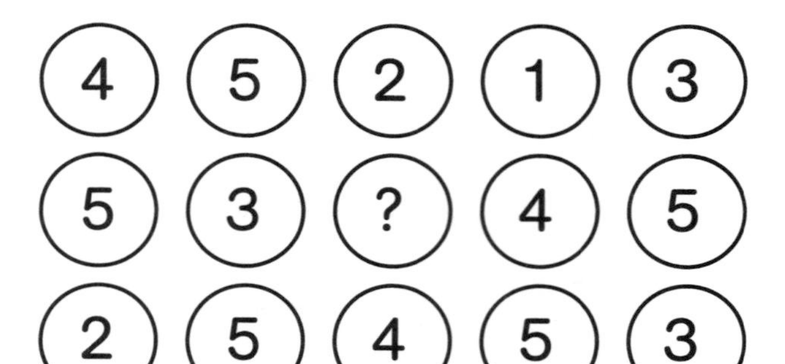

Answer Key

Games for Individuals

Baffled Boxes #1

Here are 34 words. There may also be others. dice, ding, dirt, dole, drag, drop, grid, grin, grow, iced, lord, meow, mute, nice, pled, plod, plot, plow, poem, poet, pole, rang, rice, ride, rind, ring, role, told, torn, trod, true, turn, word, worn

Baffled Boxes #2

Here are 29 possible answers. There may be others.
aimed, batch, beach, beady, beast, birch, bread, brink, camel, chant, chime, cream, earth, enter, fetch, frail, frame, heart, knead, reach, ready, scare, scarf, scent, stern, thank, trace, trade, trail

Fast Fifty

Here is one solution that uses all the numbers. There may be other solutions as well.

25 + 17 + 8
13 + 16 + 21
9 + 17 + 24
11 + 29 + 10
12 + 30 + 8
15 + 15 + 20
19 + 6 + 25
14 + 23 + 13
7 + 21 + 22
18 + 30 + 2
16 + 19 + 15
10 + 12 + 28

Logical Locations

Amber lives in Florida. Brittany lives in Tennessee.
Casey lives in Alaska. Dirk lives in South Dakota.

Are You a Divergent Thinker?

1. Here is one solution:

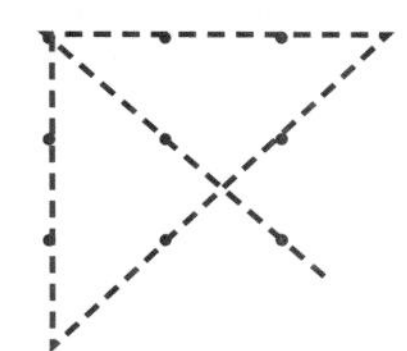

2. Place the coin that is farthest right on top of the middle coin.

3. This solution contains 4 small triangles plus 1 large one.

Tricky Treats

1. taffy apple, jellybeans, bubble gum, marshmallow chicks
2. candy bar, gumdrops, lollipop, licorice
3. candy corn, homemade fudge, rock candy, lemon drops

American Anagrams–States

1. North Carolina
2. West Virginia
3. Washington
4. Maryland
5. Colorado
6. Nebraska
7. Michigan
8. Delaware
9. New Hampshire
10. California
11. Vermont
12. Louisiana

American Anagrams–Cities

1. Raleigh
2. Milwaukee
3. Phoenix
4. Portland
5. Philadelphia
6. Sacramento
7. Detroit
8. Minneapolis
9. Charlotte
10. Providence
11. Madison
12. Houston

Toothpick Tricks
(Other answers may also be possible.)

1.

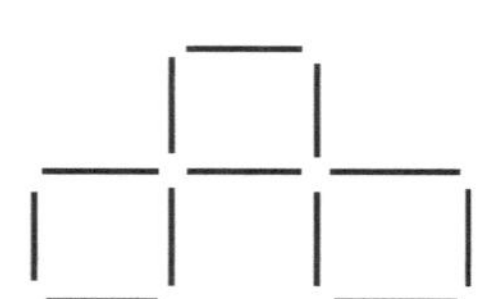

2a.

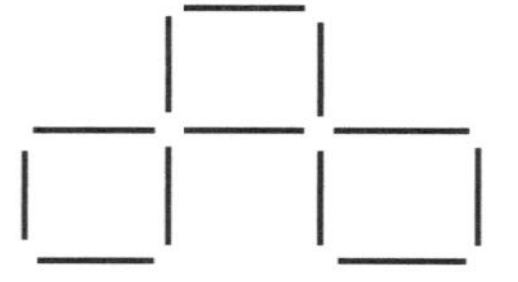

2b.

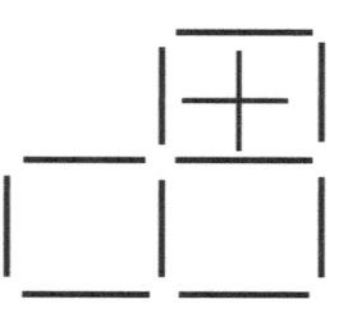

2c.

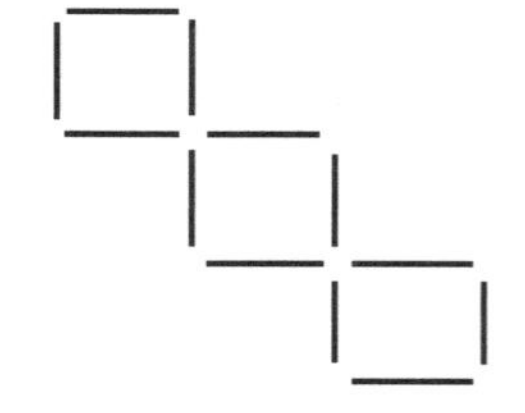

2d.

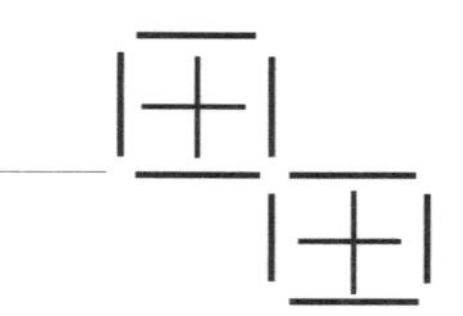

3a.

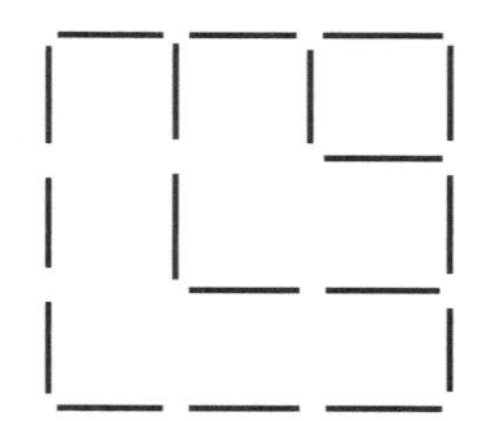

3b.

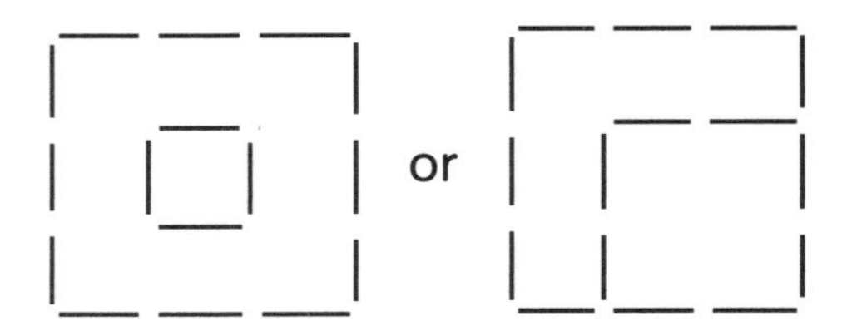

3c.

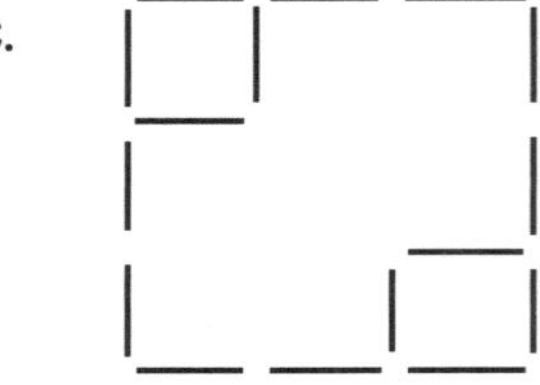

4.

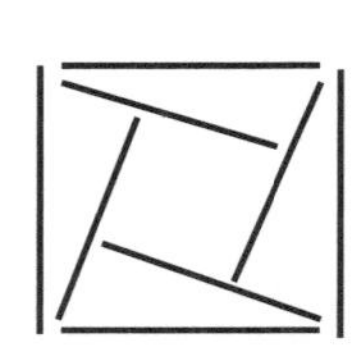

5.

6.

One At a Time
Here are some of the possible answers: bone, boom, mood, move, poem, pond, prod, reed, room, seed, seem, seer, some, term, tomb, tree, trod

Games for Individuals

Need Help?

Here are some possible solutions:
Mammals: hare, elephant, lion, porpoise
European cities: Helsinki, Edinburgh, London, Paris
Authors: (O.) Henry, (Ralph Waldo) Emerson, (Jack) London, (Edgar Allan) Poe
Birds: heron, eagle, lark, puffin
U.S. Presidents: Hoover, Eisenhower, Lincoln, Polk

Are You a Birdbrain?

1. raven; ram, venom
2. egret; egg, return
3. swan; swamp, ancient
4. thrush; throne, usher
5. robin; robot, index
6. grebe; green, beach
7. finch; final, cheap
8. eagle; each, glee
9. gull; gulf, lava
10. stork; storm, key
11. ibis; ice, bisect
12. loon; loaf, once

Phoney Numbers

1. PEA PODS
2. KEY NOTE
3. FIX LEAK
4. BIG NEWS
5. LAP TOPS
6. GET CASH
7. CUT HAIR
8. EAT LESS
9. FUN TIME
10. FITNESS

Sum Puzzlers

Here are some possible solutions:

1.

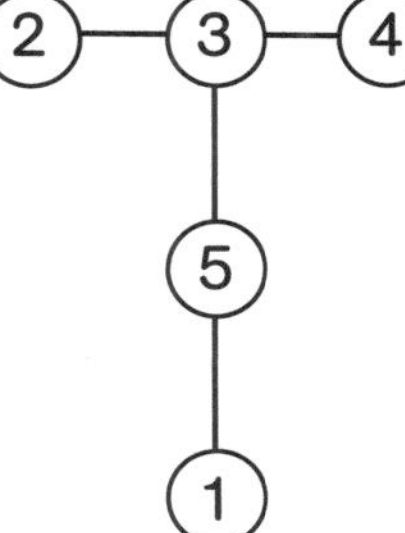

2.

10	5	12
11	9	7
6	13	8

3.

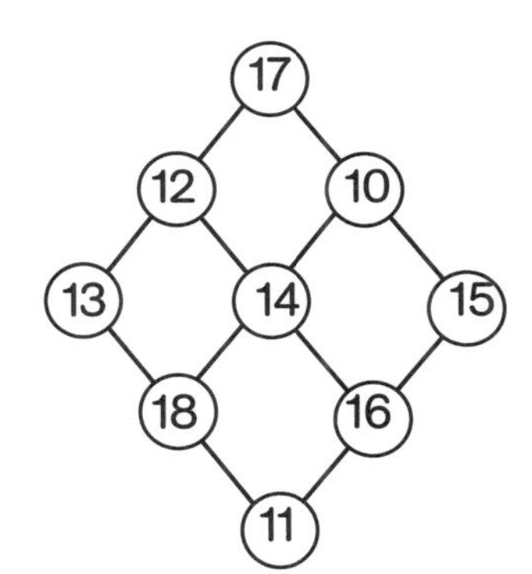

4.

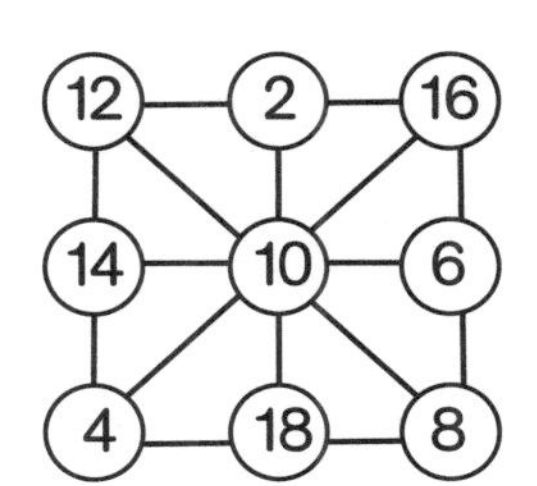

Sum: 30

Games for Individuals

Number Maze Prime Sums

Multiples of 3

10	20	3	5	6	3	12	18	2	10	16	1
15	2	27	7	1	1	3	28	15	19	13	11
31	17	4	11	2	3	9	2	1	9	2	8
11	30	9	21	8	4	4	19	26	2	14	13
33	8	12	34	29	9	32	0	11	6	16	17
10	4	10	12	30	3	27	6	7	1	20	15
18	9	3	9	24	15	6	3	0	3	19	11
6	33	36	7	3	14	5	4	18	9	6	5
5	1	14	16	5	18	13	3	1	24	3	4
7	6	11	1	5	2	21	14	0	12	36	7
23	39	9	35	8	1	10	9	2	18	6	42
12	4	13	7	18	42	2	1	4	5	9	30
15	41	36	17	15	25	16	21	3	10	19	7
6	22	16	2	40	4	7	2	12	18	6	38
14	15	13	24	3	9	8	17	4	37	1	20

Plan the Plots

This diagram allows each brother an equal share of the same size and shape with 2 trees each. Each brother will have to step into a comer of the house plot as he crosses the border diagonally.

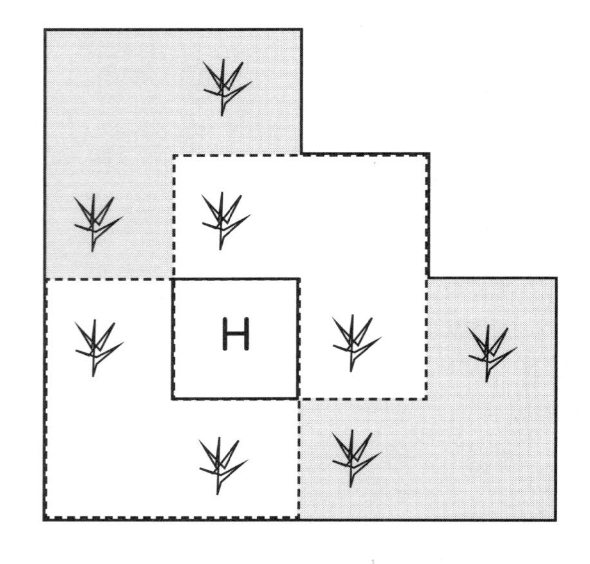

Answer Key

Games for Individuals

Relative Logic

1. D
2. E
3. B
4. G
5. A
6. J
7. H
8. F
9. K
10. I
11. D
12. C

Relative Riddles

1. 4 girls, 3 boys
2. No. A man who has a widow is a dead man.
3. With only 1 son, each daughter has a brother.
4. There were only 3 hunters: a grandfather, a son, and a grandson. So, we have 2 fathers in the grandfather and his son, and 2 sons in the son and the grandson.
5. 58 marbles
6. Sammy is 8 years old. To solve, let S = Sammy's age; M = Molly's age. We know that 4S = M. We also know that Molly must be 24 years older than Sammy, since there is a 4-year gap between each child, and there are 6 such gaps between these two. So we also can write S + 24 = M. Then 4S = S + 24, which leads to 3S = 24, and S = 8.
7. There is 1 chance in 4. Here are all the possible combinations: BBB, BBG, BGB, BGG, GBB, GGB, GGG. Each of these outcomes is equally likely. Of these, only two (BBB and GGG) are all alike. So the chances are $\frac{2}{8}$ or $\frac{1}{4}$.

Ornamental Spelling From left to right, the words are: 1. lights 2. tinsel 3. wreath 4. candle 5. ribbon 6. giving

Money Matters

1. Technically, Lola lost $12 and a pair of shoes. She kept $8 of the convenience store's "good" money, so she was only out the $12 and the shoes, not the shoes plus the entire $20.
2. Leroy is right. Here are 2 ways: a) 45 pennies, 1 quarter, 2 nickels, 2 dimes; b) 40 pennies, 8 nickels, 2 dimes.
3. From Leroy's statement it is clear that $70 was half of Monday's income. Therefore, Monday's total was $140, and Tuesday's income was $210 which yields a two-day total of $350.
4. Leroy should pay him $12.50. Sal was counting the same pairs of shoes twice. The same pairs that were on his right going back were on his left coming up.
5. Lola received $7,000. At the beginning, each person would have received $4,000. But the nephews each donated half, or $2,000 of their portion, or $6,000 between the 3 of them. Lola and the other niece then would have received an additional $3,000.
6. Dates before Christ were not written "B.C." They were only written that way after Christ lived.

Parallel Problems

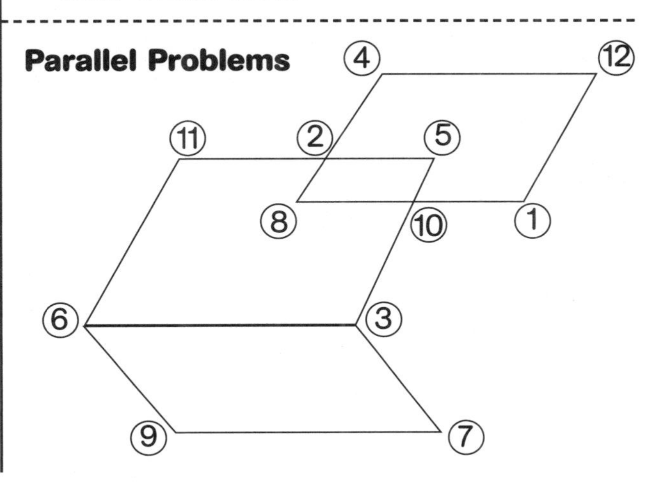

Answer Key

Games for Individuals
(Continued)

Frozen Nightmare

Here are 11 possible answers:

1. *Marvelous* is misspelled.
2. *Weight* is misspelled.
3. *You're* should be *your.*
4. Frozen food should not be stored at room temperature.
5. Package says food is made with "real beef," but the ingredients do not list it.
6. Package only contains enough for one serving, not an entire family.
7. Package says food is vitamin-fortified, but the nutrition information does not list any vitamins that it contains.
8. Package says there are no calories from fat, yet *corn oil* is listed as an ingredient.
9. The food should not take longer to heat in microwave on HIGH than it does in a conventional oven.
10. A metal sheet should not be placed in the microwave.
11. *Flower* should be *flour.*

Anatomy Code

A = L	H = O	P = M
B = I	I = Y	R = C
C = N	J = U	S = K
D = V	K = B	T = P
E = S	L = D	U = A
F = T	M = E	W = H
G = R	O = G	

1. heart
2. eye
3. brain
4. lung
5. liver
6. stomach
7. ear
8. tongue
9. kidney
10. bladder
11. intestine
12. pancreas

A Vexing Vine

1. soil
2. plant
3. seed
4. hoe
5. water
6. field
7. weed
8. grow
9. light
10. stem
11. sprout

Animal Antics

Rain, dear! (reindeer)

Places, Please

1. Here is one possible solution.

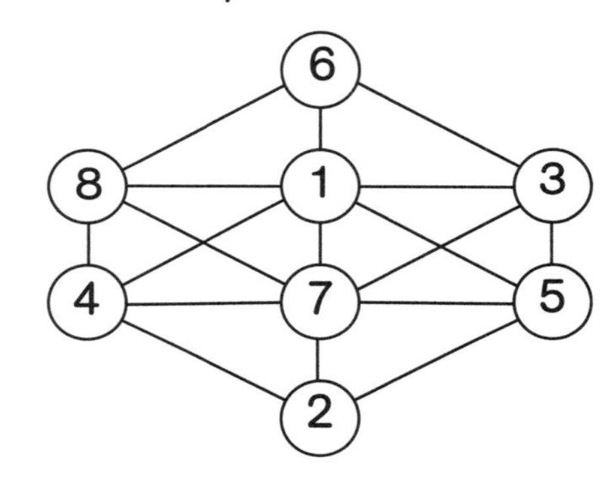

2. Here is one possible answer:

The missing number is 4, because then the puzzle will contain one 1, two 2s, three 3s, four 4s, and five 5s.

Brain Games
Partner Games

Name ______________________ Date ______________

Who can find more domino math facts, you or your opponent? To play this game, you will need an entire set of double-six or double-nine dominoes. You and your opponent will each need a pencil and a copy of pages 44 and 45.

Before you begin, be sure you know what a domino math problem looks like. In this kind of math, each half of a tile represents a digit in a math problem. For example,

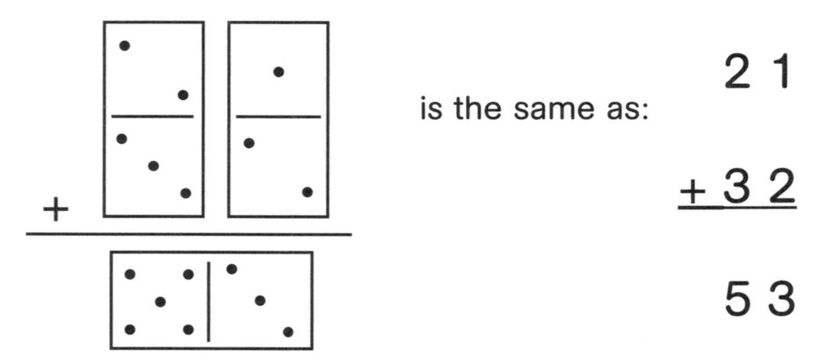

Begin by placing all the dominoes face down on the table. Decide who starts. Then each of you must, in turn, draw one domino and keep it hidden from the other player. Continue drawing dominoes one at a time until one of you can complete a domino math problem. When you are able, lay down your domino problem for your opponent to check.

When a player creates a correct math problem, that player is awarded with a point. Then return all dominos to the pile face down and begin a new round. The winner is the first person who is able to create a correct math problem or the person who makes the most problems in the alloted time.

Remember: Tiles can be read with either number in the tens spot. For instance, in the problem above, the first tile could be used as a 23 or a 32. You will want to try using all your tiles both ways in order to form a math problem quickly. Also, there are no duplicate tiles in a domino set. You would never find another 2–3 tile, so you would not be able to form the problem 23 + 32 = 55.

The next page shows other "domino math" formats you may be able to use in this game. Ask your teacher for permission before using calculators on the more difficult problems.

Name ______________________ Date ______________

Here are more ideas for constructing domino math problems. You may use any one of them on any round. There are other formats as well.

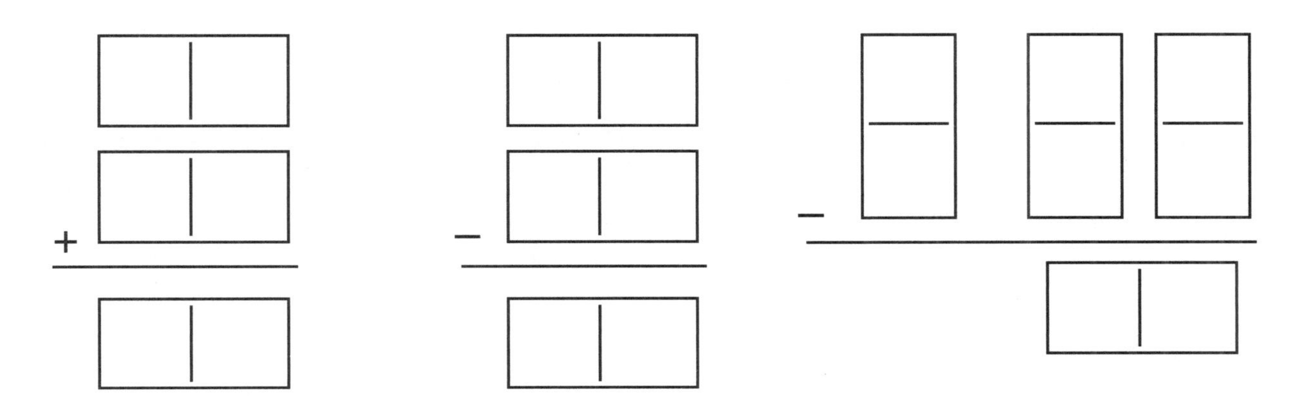

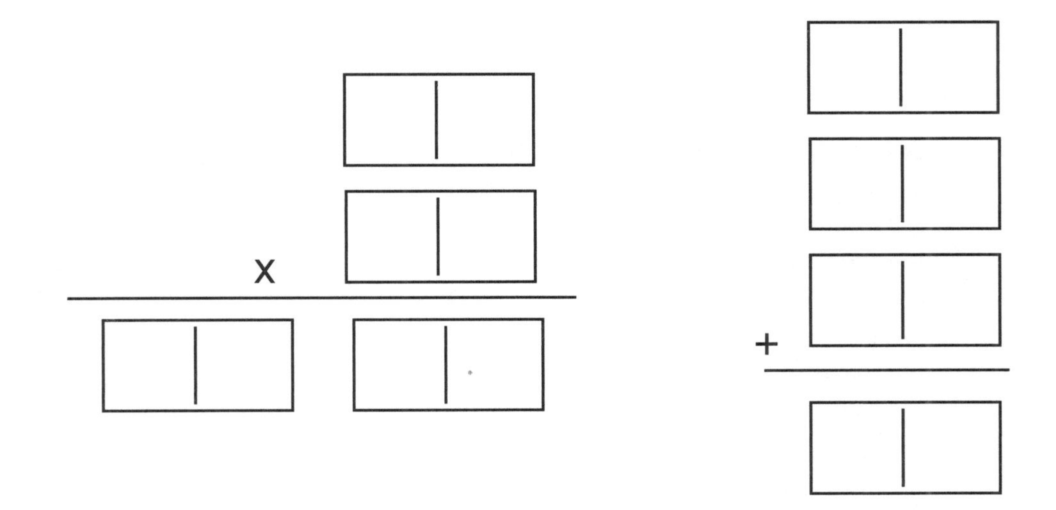

Name ______________________ Date ______________

This game will test your skills of estimating and averaging. The calculator will do the computation, but the players must do the thinking! Two to 5 people can play this game. Each player needs a calculator and 5 pennies or similar markers. The group needs 1 copy of the chart on the next page. The object is to select 5 numbers from the chart on the next page that average the target number.

To find the target number for the first round, each player must select a number between 40 and 60 and enter it into her calculator. When every player has entered a number, one player adds them all up and finds the average of the those numbers by dividing by the number of players. The resulting number is the target number. If the number is a decimal, round it to the nearest whole number.

Players clear their calculators. Play begins when the first player chooses a number from the chart, enters it on her calculator, and covers that number on the chart with a marker. The second player selects a different number from the chart, enters it on his calculator, and places a marker on it. On each player's second turn, that player selects another number and adds it to the first. Play continues in this manner until every player has entered 5 different numbers from the chart. Each player then hits the equal sign to show the total of his 5 numbers. Remember, players take turns and always mark the number used in the chart so that no number is used more than once.

When each player has had 5 turns, all of the players divide their totals by 5. The player whose answer (the average of the 5 numbers) is closest to the target number wins.

Here is how a sample game works:
Three friends each pick a number between 40 and 60. (These numbers do not need to appear on the chart.) Bryce chooses 42, Evan selects 50, and Andrew chooses 58. The average of those numbers is 50, so 50 is the target number for this game.

From the chart in the first round, Bryce selects the number 78 and covers it with a marker. Evan picks 28 and covers it, and Andrew chooses 49 and covers it. They continue in turn, choosing numbers and covering them with these results:
Bryce: $78 + 46 + 14 + 97 + 9 = 244 \div 5 = 48.8$, which rounds to 49
Evan: $28 + 61 + 83 + 89 + 2 = 263 \div 5 = 52.6$, which rounds to 53
Andrew: $49 + 69 + 74 + 33 + 43 = 268 \div 5 = 53.6$, which rounds to 54
Bryce's average of 49 is closest to 50, the target number, so he wins the first game.

Name ______________________ Date ____________

Math

Target Practice
(Continued)

46	9	94	56	33
89	43	74	5	80
24	61	42	83	2
50	49	78	28	14
69	97	36	71	17

Name ______________________ Date __________

Be the first to make perfect matches plus place things in order in this brain-stretching game for two players. Choose 1 copy of any of the Match Maker pages and cut in half. Each player gets half of the page. When 1 player completes the sequencing and all the matches, she calls out "Match Maker" and turns her paper over. Both players then compare their answers with the answer key. The player with the most correct answers wins. It is possible to be the first one to finish but not win the game, so work carefully! Use these directions for all Match Maker games.

Match Maker Plus 1–Presidents and Vice Presidents

First, number the Presidents from 1 (the earliest) to 9 (the most recent) to show the order in which they served. Place this number in the blank on the left. Then match each President with the name of one of his vice presidents. Put the letter in the blank after each President.

______1. Abraham Lincoln______
______2. Franklin D. Roosevelt______
______3. Dwight D. Eisenhower______
______4. Lyndon B. Johnson______
______5. James Garfield______
______6. Thomas Jefferson______
______7. Ronald Reagan______
______8. Andrew Jackson______
______9. William McKinley______

A. George Bush Sr.
B. Chester Arthur
C. Theodore Roosevelt
D. Hubert Humphrey
E. Andrew Johnson
F. Aaron Burr
G. Harry S. Truman
H. Martin Van Buren
I. Richard Nixon

Match Maker Plus 1–Presidents and Vice Presidents

First, number the Presidents from 1 (the earliest) to 9 (the most recent) to show the order in which they served. Put this number in the blank on the left. Then match each President with the name of one of his vice presidents. Put the letter in the blank after each President.

______1. Abraham Lincoln______
______2. Franklin D. Roosevelt______
______3. Dwight D. Eisenhower______
______4. Lyndon B. Johnson______
______5. James Garfield______
______6. Thomas Jefferson______
______7. Ronald Reagan______
______8. Andrew Jackson______
______9. William McKinley______

A. George Bush Sr.
B. Chester Arthur
C. Theodore Roosevelt
D. Hubert Humphrey
E. Andrew Johnson
F. Aaron Burr
G. Harry S. Truman
H. Martin Van Buren
I. Richard Nixon

Match Maker Plus 2–Inventions and Inventors

First, number the inventions from 1 (the earliest) to 10 (the most recent) to show the order in which they were invented. Place this number in the blank on the left. Then match each invention to its inventor. Place the letter in the blank after each invention. Some answers will be used more than once.

Invention

_______1. phonograph ______
_______2. magnifying glass______
_______3. rocket______
_______4. telephone______
_______5. dynamite______
_______6. bifocal lenses______
_______7. frozen food______
_______8. astronomical telescope______
_______9. lightning conductor______
______10. porcelain______

Inventor/Origin

A. Roger Bacon
B. Thomas Edison
C. Benjamin Franklin
D. Clarence Birdseye
E. Galileo
F. Alexander Bell
G. China
H. Alfred Nobel

Match Maker Plus 2–Inventions and Inventors

First, number the inventions from 1 (the earliest) to 10 (the most recent) to show the order in which they were invented. Place this number in the blank on the left. Then match each invention to its inventor. Place the letter in the blank after each invention. Some answers will be used more than once.

Invention

_______1. phonograph ______
_______2. magnifying glass______
_______3. rocket______
_______4. telephone______
_______5. dynamite______
_______6. bifocal lenses______
_______7. frozen food______
_______8. astronomical telescope______
_______9. lightning conductor______
______10. porcelain______

Inventor/Origin

A. Roger Bacon
B. Thomas Edison
C. Benjamin Franklin
D. Clarence Birdseye
E. Galileo
F. Alexander Bell
G. China
H. Alfred Nobel

Match Maker Plus 3—Countries and Capitals

First, number these European and African countries from 1 (the northernmost) to 9 (the southernmost) to show the order in which they are located geographically. Place this number in the blank on the left. Then match each country to its capital. Place the letter in the blank after each country.

______1. Libya______	A. Paris
______2. Finland______	B. Copenhagen
______3. South Africa______	C. Tripoli
______4. Denmark______	D. Cape Town
______5. Poland______	E. Brussels
______6. France______	F. Warsaw
______7. Sudan______	G. Madrid
______8. Spain______	H. Khartoum
______9. Belgium______	I. Helsinki

Match Maker Plus 3—Countries and Capitals

First, number these European and African countries from 1 (the northernmost) to 9 (the southernmost) to show the order in which they are located geographically. Place this number in the blank on the left. Then match each country to its capital. Place the letter in the blank after each country.

______1. Libya______	A. Paris
______2. Finland______	B. Copenhagen
______3. South Africa______	C. Tripoli
______4. Denmark______	D. Cape Town
______5. Poland______	E. Brussels
______6. France______	F. Warsaw
______7. Sudan______	G. Madrid
______8. Spain______	H. Khartoum
______9. Belgium______	I. Helsinki

Name ____ Date __________________

Match Maker Plus 4—States and Nicknames

First, number these American states from 1 (the earliest) to 10 (the latest) to show the order in which they entered the Union. Place this number in the blank on the left. Then match each state to its nickname. Place the letter in the blank after each state.

______1. Alaska_____
______2. California_____
______3. Florida_____
______4. Illinois_____
______5. Minnesota_____
______6. Nebraska_____
______7. New Mexico_____
______8. North Dakota_____
______9. Pennsylvania_____
_____10. Tennessee_____

A. Peace Garden State
B. Sunshine State
C. Cornhusker State
D. Golden State
E. Volunteer State
F. The Last Frontier
G. Gopher State
H. Keystone State
I. Prairie State
J. Land of Enchantment

Match Maker Plus 4—States and Nicknames

First, number these American states from 1 (the earliest) to 10 (the latest) to show the order in which they entered the Union. Place this number in the blank on the left. Then match each state to its nickname. Place the letter in the blank after each state.

______1. Alaska_____
______2. California_____
______3. Florida_____
______4. Illinois_____
______5. Minnesota_____
______6. Nebraska_____
______7. New Mexico_____
______8. North Dakota_____
______9. Pennsylvania_____
_____10. Tennessee_____

A. Peace Garden State
B. Sunshine State
C. Cornhusker State
D. Golden State
E. Volunteer State
F. The Last Frontier
G. Gopher State
H. Keystone State
I. Prairie State
J. Land of Enchantment

Name ______________________________ Date ______________

Shopping Spree

Congratulations! You and your partner just tied for first prize in a grocery store's contest, because you both saved $50 last month on your groceries by using coupons. Since there can be only 1 winner of the store's grand prize of a trip to Tahiti, the store is holding a tiebreaker. Here's the contest: You will both have 1 minute to go on a $100-shopping spree. You can buy any amount of any of the items shown here. You are to spend as much of the $100 as possible, but you may not spend more than $100. The person who spends the amount closest to $100 without going over that amount wins the trip to Tahiti. Write the quantity you wish to purchase under each item. You may use a calculator to find the sums quickly. Good luck!

bread–$1.29/loaf ______________	apples–69¢/lb. ______________	pork chops–$2.59/lb. ______________
milk–$2.39/gal. ______________	corn on the cob– $4.00/dozen ______________	orange juice–$2.25 per $\frac{1}{2}$ gallon ______________
frozen pizza–$6.25 ea. ______________	yogurt–44¢ ea. ______________	laundry detergent–$4.99 ea. ______________
noodles–59¢/pkg. ______________	cereal–$3.89/box ______________	ketchup–$1.89 ea. ______________

At the end of 1 minute, find your total spending amount and write it here: __________
Who wins, you or your partner?

Challenge 1 or more of your classmates to this brain-stretching-vocabulary-spelling game as you attempt some wizardry with dictionary guide words! Each of you will need one portion of the next page and a pencil. Keep your paper face down until time begins. Be certain that each of you reads and understands the rules below before beginning.

Agree with your opponent(s) on the time allowed for this game. A limit of 8 to 10 minutes is good for the first game. Set a timer or ask a friend who is not playing to keep time. On a signal, turn your papers over. List as many words as possible that could appear on a dictionary page with the guide words shown. Do not use proper nouns, plurals, the -s form of verbs (such as *eats*), or foreign words. *Do not use a dictionary!*

Scoring: Each player receives from 1 to 5 points for each word she writes. Points given for each word are shown on the gamecard in front of the guide words.

Example: 1) band–bell
Player writes: bank
bear
beckon

Player earns 1 point for each word or 3 points for this section.

Example: 2) egg–ethyl
Player writes: egret
elastic
election
elective

Player earns 2 points for each word or 8 points for this section.

Please note that you may use the back of the page or an extra sheet of paper, if you like. When time has expired, players count their points. The player with the most points wins. After scoring, players may consult a dictionary to find additional correct answers.

Make a new game card with new guide words and play another round if time permits.

Name ____________________ Date ____________

Guide Word Wizards

(Continued)

1) answer–appoint

____

____

1) coward–creek

____

____

2) gossip–grasp

____

____

2) kiln–kink

____

____

3) upset–use

____

____

3) yardstick–yellow

____

____

5) javelin–jersey

____

____

5) quarter–queen

____

____

5) zenith–zodiac

____

____

Use the back or extra paper if needed.

1) answer–appoint

____

____

1) coward–creek

____

____

2) gossip–grasp

____

____

2) kiln–kink

____

____

3) upset–use

____

____

3) yardstick–yellow

____

____

5) javelin–jersey

____

____

5) quarter–queen

____

____

5) zenith–zodiac

____

____

Use the back or extra paper if needed.

1) answer–appoint

____

____

1) coward–creek

____

____

2) gossip–grasp

____

____

2) kiln–kink

____

____

3) upset–use

____

____

3) yardstick–yellow

____

____

5) javelin–jersey

____

____

5) quarter–queen

____

____

5) zenith–zodiac

____

____

Use the back or extra paper if needed.

Name ______________________ Date ______________

Mathematical Wipe Out!

Team up with a buddy and challenge another pair of players to a game of Mathematical Wipe Out! In this game, you will work with a partner to write mathematical equations that result in as many of the answers from 1 to 25 as possible. To play, you need 2 (or more) sets of 2 players, paper and pencil, 3 dice or a spinner with at least 6 numbers, and game boards with the numbers 1–25. You also need a 3-minute timer or a stopwatch.

Pair 1 begins play by rolling the dice (or spinning the spinner 3 times). All players should jot down these 3 numbers, because these will be used in writing equations. After the third number is determined, Pair 1 starts the timer or stopwatch. Then each pair of students must work together to write as many equations as possible that result in different answers between 1 and 25. Any of the 4 operations may be used, and the numbers can appear in any order.

As each number from the game board is used, it is crossed off or "wiped out" of the chart. Play for that round ends when 3 minutes are up, or anytime before that if Pair 1 calls "stop." Of course, Pair 1 will only want to call "stop" early if they think they have more equations than their opponents.

When "stop" is called or when time has run out, both teams must stop writing. They should trade papers with another pair of students and check each others' equations. Each team then counts up the amount of numbers they have correctly wiped off their chart and are awarded 1 point for each. Continue playing with a clean game board as time allows. The pair with the most number of "wipe outs" wins.

Example:
Joe and Mo roll 3, 2, and 5. They write these equations and then call "stop."

$(3 + 5) \times 2 = 16$
$(3 - 2) \times 5 = 5$
$(5 - 2) \times 3 = 9$
$(5 - 3) + 2 = 4$
$(5 \times 3) - 2 = 13$
$(3 \times 2) + 5 = 11$
$(2 + 3) \times 5 = 25$
$(5 \times 3) + 2 = 17$
$(3 \times 2) - 51 = 46$

Flo and Bo write these equations:

$(5 \times 2) + 3 = 13$
$(2 + 3) \times 5 = 25$
$(3 + 5) \times 2 = 16$
$(3 \times 2) - 5 = 1$
$2 + 3 + 5 = 10$
$5 + (3 - 2) = 6$
$(5 - 2) \times 3 = 9$
$5 + (2 \times 3) = 11$
$(5 - 3) \times 2 = 4$
$(5 \times 3) - 2 = 13$
$(3 \times 2) + 5 = 11$
$(5 - 4) \times 3 = 3$

The 2 pairs trade papers. Joe and Mo's equations are all found to be correct. They receive 9 points. Flo and Bo have 12 equations, but the last two are not right. In the very last equation, the 4 should not be used. In the last equation in the middle column, the answer is the same as in a previous one. So this team has 10 points for this round. It is now up to Flo and Bo to roll the dice to find the next 3 numbers.

Name ______________________ Date ______________

Math

Mathematical Wipe Out!

1	2	3	4	5
6	7	8	9	10
11	12	13	14	15
16	17	18	19	20
21	22	23	24	25

1	2	3	4	5
6	7	8	9	10
11	12	13	14	15
16	17	18	19	20
21	22	23	24	25

1	2	3	4	5
6	7	8	9	10
11	12	13	14	15
16	17	18	19	20
21	22	23	24	25

1	2	3	4	5
6	7	8	9	10
11	12	13	14	15
16	17	18	19	20
21	22	23	24	25

1	2	3	4	5
6	7	8	9	10
11	12	13	14	15
16	17	18	19	20
21	22	23	24	25

1	2	3	4	5
6	7	8	9	10
11	12	13	14	15
16	17	18	19	20
21	22	23	24	25

Name ______________________ Date ______________

Grab a partner and go on a safari! In the word search on the next page, try to find one 4-letter word for each letter of the alphabet. For example, for the letter A you might find *area, acid*, or *aqua*. (Hint: One of these is the right answer.) Circle the words that you find in the word search and write them in the blanks below next to the beginning letter of the word. This will help you keep track of the words you still need to find. There is no time limit on this game. Just try to finish it with the help of a friend. If you get totally frustrated and need some hints, your teacher can provide you with a list of the words.

a ______________________

b ______________________

c ______________________

d ______________________

e ______________________

f ______________________

g ______________________

h ______________________

i ______________________

j ______________________

k ______________________

l ______________________

m ______________________

n ______________________

o ______________________

p ______________________

q ______________________

r ______________________

s ______________________

t ______________________

u ______________________

v ______________________

w ______________________

x ______________________

y ______________________

z ______________________

Name ______________________ Date ______________

Language Arts

Partner Safari

(Continued)

L	U	K	C	I	K	O	N	R	A	Y
A	Y	A	R	T	A	U	Q	I	T	A
E	T	J	I	G	A	L	O	M	S	R
V	E	A	B	A	P	R	A	X	E	X
R	P	L	T	L	M	Q	A	V	Z	I
K	O	M	I	F	U	S	E	D	O	T
N	R	M	U	A	J	E	D	F	E	J
I	B	L	Q	P	S	O	I	L	P	H
C	A	E	I	H	Z	R	E	V	O	M
E	F	I	W	E	P	O	H	S	H	G

Name ________________________ Date ______________

What's the most expensive fruit you can name? Would it be a cherry, an apple, or a plum? It is the plum, at least for this game. The letters in plum, when represented by the values shown in the lists on the following page, total 62¢ which is higher than the apple (50¢) and the cherry (52¢). To play this pricing game written for 2–5 players, you will need one copy of both this page and the next, a paper bag, a pair of scissors, a watch with a second hand, and paper and pencil for everyone.

In preparation, cut apart the categories listed on the bottom of this page and place them in the paper bag. Also cut apart the price lists on the next page and give one to each player.

Decide who will keep time for the first round. The player on the timer's right begins the game by drawing a slip of paper from the bag. That player reads this phrase aloud to the group. Each player then has 45 seconds to think of one or more words that fit the description. Players then write down the word they think has the highest or lowest value according to the chart, on their paper.

The timer announces the end of playing time, and then each player must calculate his final price. The player with the highest or lowest total (as noted on the slip of paper) wins that round. The timer then passes the watch to the player on his left, takes the paper bag from the player on his right and draws out a new slip of paper to begin another round.

Example: Luke begins by drawing a paper that reads "lowest-priced pet." He writes down *rabbit*. Josh writes *crab*. Jacinda writes *dog*. The 3 prices are: rabbit–52¢, crab–24¢, and dog–26¢. Josh wins the round by naming the lowest-priced pet.

highest-priced sport	lowest-priced item of clothing	highest-priced profession
lowest-priced pet	most expensive fruit	lowest-priced vegetable
most expensive car	lowest-priced car	highest-priced country
lowest-priced city	costliest flower	lowest-priced computer term
lowest-priced insect	highest-priced bird	lowest-priced reptile
highest-priced musical instrument	lowest-priced book title	highest-priced beverage

Name ______________________________ **Date** ________________

A = 1¢	A = 1¢	A = 1¢	A = 1¢	A = 1¢
B = 2¢	B = 2¢	B = 2¢	B = 2¢	B = 2¢
C = 3¢	C = 3¢	C = 3¢	C = 3¢	C = 3¢
D = 4¢	D = 4¢	D = 4¢	D = 4¢	D = 4¢
E = 5¢	E = 5¢	E = 5¢	E = 5¢	E = 5¢
F = 6¢	F = 6¢	F = 6¢	F = 6¢	F = 6¢
G = 7¢	G = 7¢	G = 7¢	G = 7¢	G = 7¢
H = 8¢	H = 8¢	H = 8¢	H = 8¢	H = 8¢
I = 9¢	I = 9¢	I = 9¢	I = 9¢	I = 9¢
J = 10¢	J = 10¢	J = 10¢	J = 10¢	J = 10¢
K = 11¢	K = 11¢	K = 11¢	K = 11¢	K = 11¢
L = 12¢	L = 12¢	L = 12¢	L = 12¢	L = 12¢
M = 13¢	M = 13¢	M = 13¢	M = 13¢	M = 13¢
N = 14¢	N = 14¢	N = 14¢	N = 14¢	N = 14¢
O = 15¢	O = 15¢	O = 15¢	O = 15¢	O = 15¢
P = 16¢	P = 16¢	P = 16¢	P = 16¢	P = 16¢
Q = 17¢	Q = 17¢	Q = 17¢	Q = 17¢	Q = 17¢
R = 18¢	R = 18¢	R = 18¢	R = 18¢	R = 18¢
S = 19¢	S = 19¢	S = 19¢	S = 19¢	S = 19¢
T = 20¢	T = 20¢	T = 20¢	T = 20¢	T = 20¢
U = 21¢	U = 21¢	U = 21¢	U = 21¢	U = 21¢
V = 22¢	V = 22¢	V = 22¢	V = 22¢	V = 22¢
W = 23¢	W = 23¢	W = 23¢	W = 23¢	W = 23¢
X = 24¢	X = 24¢	X = 24¢	X = 24¢	X = 24¢
Y = 25¢	Y = 25¢	Y = 25¢	Y = 25¢	Y = 25¢
Z = 26¢	Z = 26¢	Z = 26¢	Z = 26¢	Z = 26¢

Name ______________________________ Date ______________

Here's a great word game for two. You need a partner, 2 pencils, and a dictionary. Then follow these instructions:

1. Each partner selects a secret 10-letter keyword.
2. She then finds several small words that can be created with letters in that keyword. She must use each letter in the keyword at least once in the group of smaller words.
3. She then makes short, simple clues for the small words.
4. She numbers the letters in her keyword and includes them with the clues.
5. Each partner then trades clues and try to uncover her opponent's keyword.
6. The first partner to find the other's keyword is the winner.

Example:

1. Greg and Gloria decide to play Keyword. Gloria chooses TABLECLOTH as her secret keyword.

2. Using the letters in that word, she finds these smaller words: tale, blot, cot, bet, both, and tot.

3. Gloria writes these clues:

tale—a story	bet—a wager
blot—a drop of ink	both—two
cot—a simple bed	tot—a young child

4. She numbers the letters in T A B L E C L O T H and adds them to her clues.
   1 2 3 4 5 6 7 8 9 10

5. Gloria hands her clues to Greg. This is how the clues appear:
   * My 1-2-4-5 is a story.
   * My 3-4-7-8 is a drop of ink.
   * My 6-8-9 is a simple bed.
   * My 3-5-9 is a wager.
   * My 3-8-9-10 means two.
   * My 1-8-9 is a very young child.

6. Greg starts with numbered blanks and attempts to find Gloria's keyword:

____ ____ ____ ____ ____ ____ ____ ____ ____ ____
1 2 3 4 5 6 7 8 9 10

Now find a great 10-letter word and start your own Keyword game!

Name ______________________ Date ____________

Roll Fifty

For this game, you need a pair of dice, a partner, and paper and pencil for each of you. Try to beat your opponent by hitting zero as well as multiples of 50.

Each player starts with 500 points and writes that number at the top of her paper. Players take turns rolling the dice. Each person makes a 2-digit number with the numbers rolled and subtracts this number from the 500 points. The round ends when someone reaches 0. The first person to get to 0 is awarded 20 points for that round. In addition, anytime a player reaches a total that is a multiple of 50 (450, 400, 350, etc.), that player scores an additional 10 points.

For example, suppose Amy rolls a 3 and 5. She might want to make 53 and subtract that from 500, leaving a difference of 447. Her partner, Rob, rolls a 6 and 1. He might want to make 61. After he subtracts that from 500, he is left with a score of 439. However, Amy might choose to count her first roll as 35. If she subtracts that from 500, she is left with a score of 465. That leaves open the possibility that she might reach 450 on the next roll, which would give her 10 points. Likewise, Rob might choose to score his first roll as a 16, leaving him with 484 so that he, too, might hit 450 on his next roll.

Players must use strategy and take a few risks to decide whether it is best to be the first one to reach 0 or to reach as many multiples of 50 as possible. Remember, the round ends when one player reaches 0. The player with the most points at the end of the round is the winner.

Name ____________________ Date ____________

Play this game to learn who can estimate distances the best–you or an opponent. Each of you should estimate these distances first and write your guesses in the blanks. You can decide if you are using metric units of measurement or American units. Also decide the units of measure to be used for each object. When measuring objects, be sure you are both making estimates for the same exact item. Then get out the ruler and measure each length. Give a point to the person who is closest for each item. Then count up your points to see who wins the round.

Names:	Player 1	Player 2
1. The width of your desk	________	________
2. The distance from the floor to the top of your desk	________	________
3. The height of the classroom door	________	________
4. The distance between the tip of your thumb and the tip of your pinky when your hand is outstretched	________	________
5. The length of your opponent's foot	________	________
6. The length of a pencil	________	________
7. Width of computer case	________	________
8. Height of computer monitor	________	________
9. Thickness of a classroom reference book	________	________
10. Width of chalkboard or bulletin board	________	________
11. Perimeter of classroom poster	________	________
Final score:	________	________

For another challenge, play Who Rules?–Round 2 on the next page!

If you and your opponent are ready for a rematch, try this "timely" challenge. You will need a stopwatch or a watch with a second hand. Again, each of you should write your estimates in the blanks below. Then perform each task and measure the actual time required for each one. Only 1 person needs to perform each task. Take turns doing the task and watching the time. Award a point to the player whose estimate was closest to the actual time. Then count up your points to see who wins the round.

Names:	Player 1	Player 2
1. The length of time it takes you to walk leisurely around the outer edge of your classroom	__________	__________
2. The time it takes you to quickly recite the alphabet	__________	__________
3. The time it takes you to walk at a normal pace to the school library and back	__________	__________
4. The time it takes to read aloud the Preamble to the U.S. Constitution	__________	__________
5. The time it takes to count aloud to 100 quickly	__________	__________
6. The time it takes to walk to your teacher's desk and back	__________	__________
7. The time it takes to tie a pair of shoelaces	__________	__________
8. The time it takes to count by 5s to 200	__________	__________
9. The time it takes to walk to the pencil sharpener, sharpen a pencil, and walk back to your seat	__________	__________
10. The time it takes to recite the alphabet backwards	__________	__________
11. The time it takes to read aloud all the words on this page	__________	__________
Final Score:	__________	__________

Name ________________________ Date ______________

How long of a chain can you make with compound words? Here is a game to test your knowledge of compound words and your skill in linking them together. To play, you need to have another player, a piece of paper, and a pencil.

The first player calls out or writes down a compound word, such as *uphill.* The second player then makes a new word using the second part of the previous word. In this case, his word could be *hillside.* Then the first player might make the word *sidewalk* and play continues on. If Player 2 is unable to add a word to the chain, Player 1 may continue the chain if he is able. The game is over when neither player is able to add a word to the chain.

Scoring: Each player receives 1 point for each word he or she adds to the chain. The player who adds the last word receives a 2-point bonus. The winner is the player with the most points.

Here is an example of how the game is played and scored:

Player 1: uphill	1 point
Player 2: hillside	1 point
Player 1: sidewalk	1 point
Player 2: no answer	0 point
Player 1: walkway	1 point
Player 2: wayward	1 point
Player 1: no answer	0 point
Player 2: wardrobe	1 point + 2-point bonus
Player 1: no answer	
Player 2: no answer	
End of game	

Final score: Player 1–3 points, Player 2–5 points

Name ______________________ Date ______________

While the world's population is constantly increasing, different regions of the world experience different rates of growth. Weather, natural resources, disease, and widespread disasters are just some of the reasons for differing growth rates. In this game you will estimate the future population in certain places. You will need 2 or more players, a recent almanac (or information from the Internet), 1 calculator for the group, and paper and pencil for each player.

To play this game, the group must first select a country for which you can obtain current information. The group needs either to find the actual rate of growth for the country, or agree upon a growth rate that seems reasonable. Each player then studies the population and growth rate briefly and writes down a guess about the estimated population of the country's population 10 years from now.

Next, a person from the group uses the calculator to find the future population. Here is an easy way to find it:

- Enter the growth rate (1.03, for instance, if the growth rate is 3%) followed by the multiplication sign. It is important to enter this first before the population number.
- Next, enter the current population of the country by the number of thousands or millions. (In other words, if the population is 356 million, the correct entry would be 356. For smaller countries, the number of thousands would be entered.)
- Finally, press the = key ten times. The display will show the population of the country in 10 years.

The player whose guess comes closest to the calculator's projected answer is the winner. The winner is allowed to select the country for the next round.

Example: The group decides to learn about the African country of Ethiopia. An almanac shows the population of Ethiopia for a recent year was about 58,000,000 and its growth rate was about 2%. The first player, Hannah, guesses that in 10 years, the population of Ethiopia will be about 65 million. Betsy guesses that it will be about 72 million. Silvia guesses it will be about 75 million. One of the girls keys in the growth rate and population according to the directions above. Rounded to two decimal places, these are the numbers shown on the calculator's display after the equals sign is pressed each time: 59.16, 60.34, 61.55, 62.78, 64.04, 65.32, 66.62, 67.96, 69.32, 70.70. So Betsy's guess of 72 million was the closest. She is allowed to choose the next country.

Variation: You may also play this game with cities or states.

Name ______________________ Date ______________

Find a buddy and then challenge another pair of players to be "chart smart." Try to be the first team to complete this A–Z chart. Here is how to play: First choose 3 categories to write at the top of the chart in the blanks. Then, with your partner, work as quickly as you can writing words in each blank. You will want to write in pencil in case you need to erase a category and start over.

For example, if you picked U.S. cities as a category, you might write *Annapolis, Baltimore,* and *Cleveland* in the first 3 lines. Continue working until 1 team has filled in every blank. The winning team is the one who has 26 correct answers for each of their 3 categories or the team with the most correct answers when time runs out.

Categories	______	______	______
A			
B			
C			
D			
E			
F			
G			
H			
I			
J			
K			
L			
M			
N			
O			
P			
Q			
R			
S			
T			
U			
V			
W			
X			
Y			
Z			

Name ______________________ Date ______________

How quickly can you hook a dozen fish? Challenge a classmate to go fishing with you in this quick game. Each player gets half of this page. Beginning at the same time, both players should race to see who can unscramble the names of these 12 types of fish. Write the answers in the blank spaces provided.

1. creph ______________
2. uttor ______________
3. noalms ______________
4. winmon ______________
5. shiftac ______________
6. plidnoh ______________
7. nuat ______________
8. hrask ______________
9. grenhir ______________
10. lestm ______________
11. pransep ______________
12. dachkod ______________

---

1. creph ______________
2. uttor ______________
3. noalms ______________
4. winmon ______________
5. shiftac ______________
6. plidnoh ______________
7. nuat ______________
8. hrask ______________
9. grenhir ______________
10. lestm ______________
11. pransep ______________
12. dachkod ______________

Name ______________________ Date ______________

How many correct answers can you find to some tough questions in just 2 minutes?

Gather a group of 2 or more students together and find out!

Prepare:

- You need a copy of this page and the next. Cut apart the cards and place them face down on a table.
- Be certain each player has plenty of paper and a pencil.
- Each player is allowed to have one reference book of choice.
- Locate a 2-minute hour-glass timer, a stopwatch, or a watch with a second hand.
- Decide who goes first. Player A may choose the first card from the pile and Player B can watch the timer. For the next round, Player B may draw the card and Player C (or Player A if only two are playing) may monitor the time.

Play:

- Player A selects the first question from the pile and reads it aloud to the group. The timekeeper says "Go," and players write as many answers as possible before the timekeeper says, "Stop."
- When time is up, students compare answers and consult the answer key if necessary.
- Award one point to the player(s) with the most correct answers.
- Play more rounds as time allows.

1. List the 2-letter postal abbreviations for the states in the U.S.	4. List foods commonly eaten as vegetables that are not green.
2. List words containing a double **o**, as in *bloom.*	5. List U.S. cities that have names of 2 words, such as San Francisco.
3. List idioms that refer to a part of the body, such as, "We don't see eye to eye on this."	6. List mammals with names that begin with the letter S.

Name ______________________ Date ____________

Problem Solving

Two-Minute Teasers

(Continued)

7. List specific types of doctors, such as *pediatrician*. Be ready to tell each one's specialty.

8. List prime numbers between 50 and 150.

9. List the keys on a computer keyboard that are not numbers or letters.

10. List units of measurement that are used to label volume.

11. Write the first, middle, and last names of any former U.S. president for which you can remember all 3 names.

12. Name events traditionally held during the Winter Olympic Games.

13. List musical instruments that are not played by mouth.

14. List holidays and special observances that occur in the first 6 months of the calendar year.

15. List books in which the main characters are animals.

16. List the names of mountain ranges around the world.

17. List the names of South American countries.

18. List the names of Asian cities.

19. List the names of European rivers.

20. List the names of major islands.

Can you make sense of number sets that your challenger writes? Play this brain-stretching game in which you will try both to trick your opponent and solve the puzzling problems he presents. The only thing you need for this game is paper, pencil, an opponent, and some sharp thinking!

Look at this box of numbers. The numbers may at first seem to be completely random. But if you look more closely, you can find that the numbers fall into two different sets. The first set is made of factors of 100: 2, 5, 10, 25, and 50. The second set is made of consecutive numbers in the thirties: 31, 32, 33, 34, and 35.

		33		10
2			25	
	32			5
		50	31	35
34				

Now that you have the idea, you and your opponent can make boxed number sets for each other to solve. Think of 2 number patterns to use for each box. Find 5 numbers that belong to each set, and then put the 10 numbers together in one box. You may want to make some adjustments once you see how they all look when put together.

Trade papers with your opponent. Under your opponent's box, write a brief description of the patterns you find and list the numbers that belong in each set. See who can be the first to identify both number patterns in the box and sort the numbers into sets correctly. The player that first makes sense of the number sets in the box is the winner.

One word of caution: There may occasionally be more than 1 way to sort the numbers that you write. Your opponent may see a number pattern that you didn't know was there!

Name ______________________ Date ______________

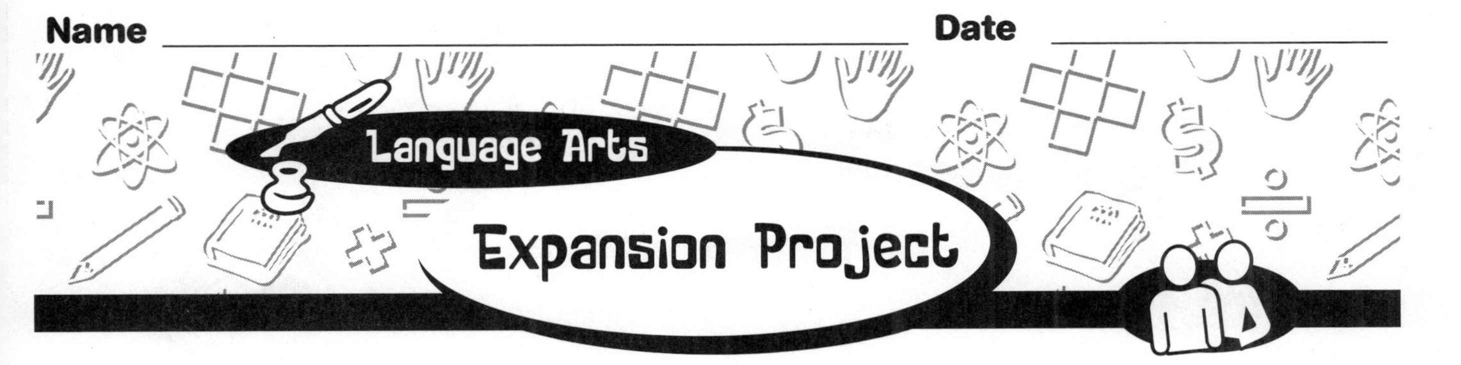

Try to outstretch your opponent in this fun word-building game. Compete with a partner to see who can add the most letters to a 3-letter word. Here is how to play:

- Decide how much time each player will be allowed to add a letter and expand the word. A time limit of 30–60 seconds is suggested in order to keep the game moving along, although players may agree on a longer time if they choose. Begin with any 3-letter word.
- Take turns adding a letter to create a larger word.
- On each turn, players are allowed to rearrange letters in any way they choose.
- Proper names and foreign words may not be used.
- The last player to add a letter is the winner of that round.
- Players may use dictionaries, provided they can complete a word within the time limit.

Example:

1. Player I selects any 3-letter word.	rat
2. Player 2 adds a letter to form a 4-letter word.	part
3. Player 1 adds another letter.	party
4. Player 2 adds a letter.	pastry
5. Player I cannot think of a way to add a letter.	
6. Player 2 wins the round.	

Here are some 3-letter words to help you get started. You will notice that some are easier to expand than others.

sat	and	day	ago	dog	buy
hen	out	how	her	dew	far
see	one	for	cat	pig	use
may	new	say	air	ill	pit
end	pal	gas	hum	sly	lad
try	toy	did	man	red	sir

Name ______________________ Date ______________

Challenge a friend to see who can travel the longest distance on a trip within the continental United States. This game is similar to one you may have played before, but with an added educational twist. You will need another player, a map of the U.S. that includes a mileage scale, a game card from the next page, and a pencil.

For this game, the distances measured will be "as the crow flies." You will need to measure the shortest distances between 2 cities using a straight line—much like a bird or an airplane would fly. Do not use road mileage guides included with many road maps and atlases. Also, all cities named should be within the continental United States.

Player 1 begins by naming any city within the 48 contiguous states. Player 2 jots down the name of that city. Player 2 must then name a new city that begins with the last letter of the first city. Player 1 then writes down the name of that city. Play continues until each player has written 7 cities on his page. Now the real work begins!

Each player must determine the distance he would travel if he visited each of the seven cities on his paper in the order they are listed. Fill in the approximate mileage on the game card as indicated between each city, and then find the grand total. The player with the higher mileage wins!

- A player should watch his opponent's game card and, whenever possible, try to name a city relatively close to the last city on his list.
- Players must keep game cards clearly visible during the game.
- Players may notice that many states have cities that share the same name. When calculating mileage on the score card, players may choose any of these cities.

Example:
Player 1: Denver
Player 2 (must name a city that begins with R): Raleigh
Player 1: Harrisburg
Player 2: Galveston
Player 1: New Orleans
Player 2: Seattle

The beginning of Player 1's game card would look like this:

Denver
} 1450
Harrisburg
} 1100
New Orleans

Name ______________________________ Date ______________

Game Cards for "Travel Log"

Player's Name: ______________

	City	Miles between
1.	________	
		} ________
2.	________	
		} ________
3.	________	
		} ________
4.	________	
		} ________
5.	________	
		} ________
6.	________	
		} ________
7.	________	
	Total:	________

Player's Name: ______________

	City	Miles between
1.	________	
		} ________
2.	________	
		} ________
3.	________	
		} ________
4.	________	
		} ________
5.	________	
		} ________
6.	________	
		} ________
7.	________	
	Total:	________

Player's Name: ______________

	City	Miles between
1.	________	
		} ________
2.	________	
		} ________
3.	________	
		} ________
4.	________	
		} ________
5.	________	
		} ________
6.	________	
		} ________
7.	________	
	Total:	________

Player's Name: ______________

	City	Miles between
1.	________	
		} ________
2.	________	
		} ________
3.	________	
		} ________
4.	________	
		} ________
5.	________	
		} ________
6.	________	
		} ________
7.	________	
	Total:	________

Name ______________________ Date ______________

In this game of chance and strategy, you will try to be the one who gets the lucky draw, with all the right numbers drawn at just the right time! The object is to have the highest total at the end of the round. Play this game with 2 to 4 players.

First, prepare the cards that you will be drawing. Use small index cards or slips of paper cut to about the same size. You will need 20 cards. Make 2 sets of cards numbered from 0 to 9. Place these numbered cards in a paper sack or other similar container.

Next, prepare your game sheet. It is shown on the next page. You will want to play several rounds, so be certain you have several copies of the next page. To begin, make sure each of you has space to record at least 3 rounds.

Finally, learn the rules.

- Player A draws a card from the 20-card set. He decides where he wants to place it on his game sheet. It becomes a missing factor for one equation. Player A does not replace that card in the bag.
- Player A continues drawing one card at a time and recording the number in a box on his game sheet. When he has drawn 7 cards and filled in all the boxes, he returns all the cards to the bag and passes the bag to Player B.
- Player B (and every player after her) follows the same directions. When the last player has completed his or her game sheet, all players should find their totals and compare results. The player with the highest total wins the round.
- For the next round, let Player B draw first.

Naturally, players will try to predict when they will draw the higher numbers so they can pair them with the higher factors on their game sheets. Remember there are two of every digit from 0 to 9 when making these predictions. Beware of the zero!

Name ______________________ Date ____________

Game sheets

Player: ____________
1 x ☐ = ________
2 x ☐ = ________
3 x ☐ = ________
4 x ☐ = ________
5 x ☐ = ________
6 x ☐ = ________
10 x ☐ = ________
Total: ________

Player: ____________
1 x ☐ = ________
2 x ☐ = ________
3 x ☐ = ________
4 x ☐ = ________
5 x ☐ = ________
6 x ☐ = ________
10 x ☐ = ________
Total: ________

Player: ____________
1 x ☐ = ________
2 x ☐ = ________
3 x ☐ = ________
4 x ☐ = ________
5 x ☐ = ________
6 x ☐ = ________
10 x ☐ = ________
Total: ________

Player: ____________
1 x ☐ = ________
2 x ☐ = ________
3 x ☐ = ________
4 x ☐ = ________
5 x ☐ = ________
6 x ☐ = ________
10 x ☐ = ________
Total: ________

Player: ____________
1 x ☐ = ________
2 x ☐ = ________
3 x ☐ = ________
4 x ☐ = ________
5 x ☐ = ________
6 x ☐ = ________
10 x ☐ = ________
Total: ________

Player: ____________
1 x ☐ = ________
2 x ☐ = ________
3 x ☐ = ________
4 x ☐ = ________
5 x ☐ = ________
6 x ☐ = ________
10 x ☐ = ________
Total: ________

No section of games for partners would be complete without the time-honored games of Hangman, Checkers, and Boxes. Here a few suggestions for incorporating the popularity and fun of these games with educational content.

Hangman

Almost everyone is familiar with this fun word game. Add your own educational twist by requiring more from students than just solving the mystery word. Here are some suggestions:

Vocabulary in any subject area—If a student solves the word, he or she must also be able to define it and/or use it correctly in a sentence.

Geography—If a student finds the name of a city, he or she must also be able to name the state or country in which it is located.

Assign partners to play against each other. Decide if you will specify what content area students should work on. Then give these instructions:

Player 1 thinks of a word. She draws one blank for every letter in the word, along with the gallows as shown here. Player 2 guesses a letter. If the letter is in the word, Player 1 writes it in the appropriate blank (or blanks, if it appears more than once in the word). If the letter is not in the word, a portion of a stick man is drawn.

Play continues until Player 2 solves the word or until the player's "man" is hung. Remember to require the player to do more than just solve the word. He must also be able to define the word and give its location.

Students should agree before play begins on exactly how many parts can be drawn before the man is hung. In order, here are 8 parts that students could use for drawing their men: head, body, right leg, left leg, right arm, left arm, right eye, left eye.

The partner who has solved the most words when time expires is the winner.

Name ______________________ Date ____________

Checkers

Use a standard checkerboard and checkers, following normal rules for making jumps. In order to make more checkerboards available, so that several pairs of students may play simultaneously, reproduce the checkerboard on the following page. Also have each player cut out 12 markers from construction paper in a color that will be different from that of the opponent.

Add this "educational" twist:
Before a game begins, assign the 2 players a list of spelling words. When a player makes a jump, he must correctly spell a word from the pre-selected list. His opponent chooses the word. If the player on the offensive correctly spells the word, he removes his opponent's checker. If he cannot spell it, his opponent's checker remains on the board and he returns his checker to its former position.

Boxes

In this game, players take turns drawing lines to connect dots. When a player is able to make the last side of a square and thus complete a "box," she writes her initial inside. Students may draw their own gameboards or use the one shown on the next page. Add one of these requirements before a player is allowed to draw a line:

Use a deck of cards listed below, shuffled and placed face down. The first player takes the top card. If she answers it correctly, she draws a line. If she is incorrect, she does not draw a line and the second player then takes a turn.

- Multiplication flashcards—give the correct product
- Equations—give the correct answer. [Ex: (4 x 5) + (6 ÷ 3). Answer: 22]
- Vocabulary words—give the correct definition
- U.S. states—give the capital, nickname, or other information
- U.S. Presidents—name one of his vice presidents
- Authors—name one of his/her works

Play continues until time is expired or the gameboard is full. Each player is awarded 1 point for each box containing her initial or 3 points if the box contains a star. The player with more points wins.

Name ______________________ Date ____________

Checkerboard

Name ______________________ Date ______________

Student Page

Boxes

Total points for Player 1: ____________ Total points for Player 2: ____________

Total points for Player 1: ____________ Total points for Player 2: ____________

Answer Key
Partner Games

Match Maker Plus

1–Presidents and Vice Presidents

1. Lincoln, 3, E
2. Roosevelt, 6, G
3. Eisenhower, 7, I
4. Johnson, 8, D
5. Garfield, 4, B
6. Jefferson, 1, F
7. Reagan, 9, A
8. Jackson, 2, H
9. McKinley, 5, C

2–Inventions and Inventors

1. phonograph, 9, B
2. magnifying glass, 3, A
3. rocket, 2, G
4. telephone, 8, F
5. dynamite, 7, H
6. bifocal lenses, 6, C
7. frozen food, 10, D
8. astronomical telescope, 4, E
9. lightning conductor, 5, C
10. porcelain, 1, G

3–Countries and Capitals

1. Libya, 7, C
2. Finland, 1, I
3. South Africa, 9, D
4. Denmark, 2, B
5. Poland, 4, F
6. France, 5, A
7. Sudan, 8, H
8. Spain, 6, G
9. Belgiun 3, E

4–States and Nicknames

1. Alaska, 10, F
2. California, 5, D
3. Florida, 4, B
4. Illinois, 3, I
5. Minnesota, 6, G
6. Nebraska, 7, C
7. New Mexico, 9, J
8. North Dakota, 8, A
9. Pennsylvania, 1, H
10. Tennessee, 2, E

Shopping Spree

Here is a sample outcome that costs $99.88:

Qty	Item	Cost
4	pizzas	25.00
3	milks	7.17
8	cereals	31.12
2	detergents	9.98
4	pork chops	10.36
1	doz. corn	4.00
2	bread loaves	2.58
10	apples	6.90
2	yogurts	.88
1	ketchup	+ 1.89
Total		$99.88

Partner Games

Partner Safari

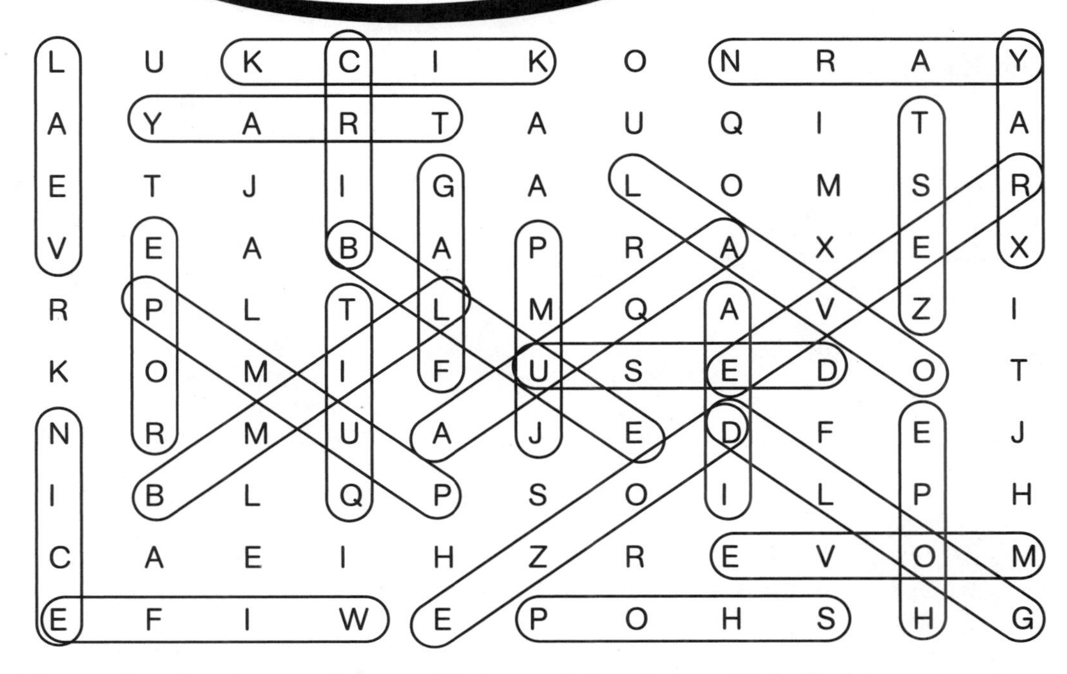

Word List: aqua, blue, crib, doze, ever, flag, gold, hope, idea, jump, kick, limb, move, nice, oval, pump, quit, rope, shop, tray, used, veal, wife, x-ray, yarn, zest. (Variations may also be possible.)

Chart Smarts

Here are some possible answers:

1. U.S. Cities: Annapolis, Baltimore, Cleveland, Dallas, Evanston, Frankfort, Gary, Hartford, Indianapolis, Jackson, Kalamazoo, Lansing, Minneapolis, New York City, Oklahoma City, Pittsburgh, Quincy, Richmond, Seattle, Tallahassee, Union City, Ventura, Washington, D.C., There is no city for the letter X, Youngstown, Zanesville
2. Foods: artichokes, beets, carrots, devil's food cake, eggs, fudge, goulash, ham, ice cream, jelly, kale, lettuce, milk, nuts, oranges, pancakes, quiche, raspberries, steak, turnips, udo, vanilla milkshake, waffle, there is no food for the letter x, yam, Zwieback toast.
3. Boys' Names: Aaron, Brian, Charles, David, Edward, Fred, Greg, Harold, Ivan, James, Kyle, Leonard, Matthew, Nathan, Owen, Paul, Quentin, Russell, Sam, Thomas, Uriah, Vernon, Wade, Xavier, York, Zachary.

Something's Fishy

1. perch
2. trout
3. salmon
4. minnow
5. catfish
6. dolphin
7. tuna
8. shark
9. herring
10. smelt
11. snapper
12. haddock

Partner Games

Two-Minute Teasers

1. Postal codes, alphabetically by state name: AL, AK, AZ, AR, CA, CO, CT, DE, FL, GA, HI, ID, IL, IN, IA, KS, KY, LA, ME, MD, MA, MI, MN, MS, MO, MT, NE, NV, NH, NJ, NM, NY, NC, ND, OH, OK, OR, PA, RI, SC, SD, TN, TX, UT, VT, VA, WA, WV, WI, WY

2. Sample oo words: school, pool, spool, fool, food, blood, hood, loom, room, groom, zoom, roof, goof, proof, hoot, balloon, maroon, etc.

3. Possible idioms include: *Stop pulling my leg; Try to keep your head; Get off my back; Does the cat have your tongue?; Please lend me a hand; Get out of my hair; He has a green thumb.*

4. Answers include: corn, carrots, beets, radishes, cauliflower, potatoes, onions, parsnips, turnips, etc.

5. San Diego, Los Angeles, Carson City, Fort Worth, Wichita Falls, Cedar Rapids, New Orleans, Baton Rouge, Kansas City, Des Moines, Daytona Beach, etc.

6. Possible answers include: squirrel, skunk, sheep, shrew, seal, sea lion, etc.

7. Sample answers include: allergist, anesthesiologist, cardiologist, dermatologist, gerontologist, hematologist, neurologist, ophthamologist, orthopedist, orthodontist, plastic surgeon, and so on.

8. 53, 59, 61, 67, 71, 73, 79, 83, 89, 97, 101, 103, 107, 109, 113, 127, 131, 137, 139, 149.

9. Possible answers include: enter, backspace, tab, control, shift, caps, lock, alt, escape, insert, delete, etc. Check a computer for more.

10. Possible answers include: cubic inches, cubic feet, cubic yards, teaspoons, tablespoons, cups, pints, quarts, gallons, pecks, bushels, milliliters, liters, cubic millimeters, cubic centimeters, etc.

11. Here is one list. Other sources may provide additional names. John Quincy Adams, William Henry Harrison, James Knox Polk, Ulysses Simpson Grant, Rutherford Birchard Hayes, James Abram Garfield, Chester Alan Arthur, Stephen Grover Cleveland, William Howard Taft, Thomas Woodrow Wilson, Warren Gamaliel Harding, John Calvin Coolidge, Herbert Clark Hoover, Franklin Delano Roosevelt, Dwight David Eisenhower, John Fitzgerald Kennedy, Lyndon Baines Johnson, Richard Milhous Nixon, Gerald Rudolph Ford, James Earl Carter, Jr., Ronald Wilson Reagan, George Herbert Walker Bush, William Jefferson Clinton, George Walker Bush.

12. Possible answers include: men's and women's figure skating, speed skating, alpine skiing and freestyle skiing, ice hockey, luge, snowboarding, bobsledding, curling, biathlon.

13. Answers include: piano, violin, viola, cello, guitar, banjo, drums, cymbals, xylophone, chimes, tambourine, triangle, etc.

14. Answers include: New Year's Day, Martin Luther King, Jr., Day, Groundhog Day, Presidents Day, Valentine's Day, Ash Wednesday, St. Patrick's Day, Easter, Mother's Day, Memorial Day, Flag Day, Father's Day, and many more.

15. Possible answers include: *Animal Farm, Watership Down, Babar the Elephant, Winnie-the-Pooh, Curious George,* and many, many more.

16.– 20. Consult an atlas to check your answers on these.

Brain Games
Games for the Entire Class

Name ______________________ Date ______________

As the name implies, in this game students will try to find pairs of items. Players will turn over 2 squares at a time as they try to pair various items. Since there are 36 squares on each game board, students will need to concentrate in order to remember where items are placed. Making a match depends on players' memories! We are including 3 sample game boards for your convenience. Once you have the idea, you can prepare more of your own on any topic!

For this game, you will need an overhead projector, a teacher-prepared transparency of the game boards, and small cardboard squares to cover the grid sections on the transparency.

Divide the class into 2 teams. Let 1 player from the first team come to the projector and carefully turn over any 2 squares. If the revealed items go together, that team scores 1 point, and that player is allowed to select 2 more squares. The matching squares are not recovered. If the 2 squares are not a match, the squares are hidden again. Then a player from the opposing team comes to the projector and turns over 2 squares of his choice. Continue playing in the same manner until the entire game board has been cleared. The team with the most matches wins.

Here are some ideas (in addition to those featured on the following pages) for possible variations of this fun whole-class game.

Math
Match equivalent metric measurements (such as 18 cm = 180 mm).
Match lists of prime factors with their product (such as $2^2 \times 3 \times 5 = 60$).

Social Studies
Match Presidents with vice presidents, election years, nicknames, or wives' first names. Match states with capitals, nicknames, or mottos. Match explorers with territories explored.

Science
Match inventors with inventions. Match animals with names of male/female/young. Match chemical elements with their symbols.

Language Arts
Match literature titles with authors.
Match abbreviations with words.

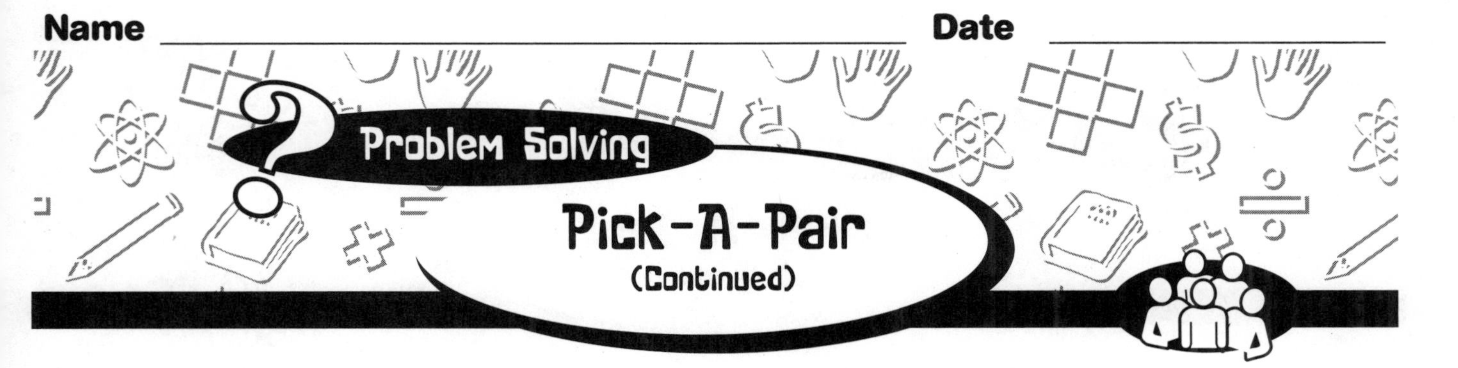

Animal Groups

Match the animal to its group name. For example, a group of gorillas is called a band, so match *gorillas* with *band*. Note: Some group names appear twice for 2 different animal groups.

kittens	band	brood	horses	troop	gorillas
seals	lions	litter	elephants	bed	hens
swarm	pigs	kangaroos	locusts	geese	yoke
ants	colony	fish	team	flock	flock
litter	pod	bees	herd	pride	wolves
school	pack	plague	clams	oxen	sheep

Name ______________________ Date ______________

Greek and Roman Gods and Goddesses

Match the god or goddess to his/her connection to mythology. For example, Nemesis is the Greek goddess of vengeance, so match *Nemesis* with *vengeance*. Note: Some specialties appear twice for 2 different gods/goddesses.

Poseidon	Athena	Helios	earth	Nemesis	sea
moon	Zeus	fire	love	Cupid	sun
Persephone	death and/or the underworld	sun	spring	Ares	queen of gods
love	Zeus	dreams/ sleep	Eros	Luna	Mercury
thunder	Hades	Somnus	wisdom	Terra	vengeance
Apollo	king of Gods	war	Vulcan	Hera	messenger/ science/ invention

Name ______________________ Date ____________

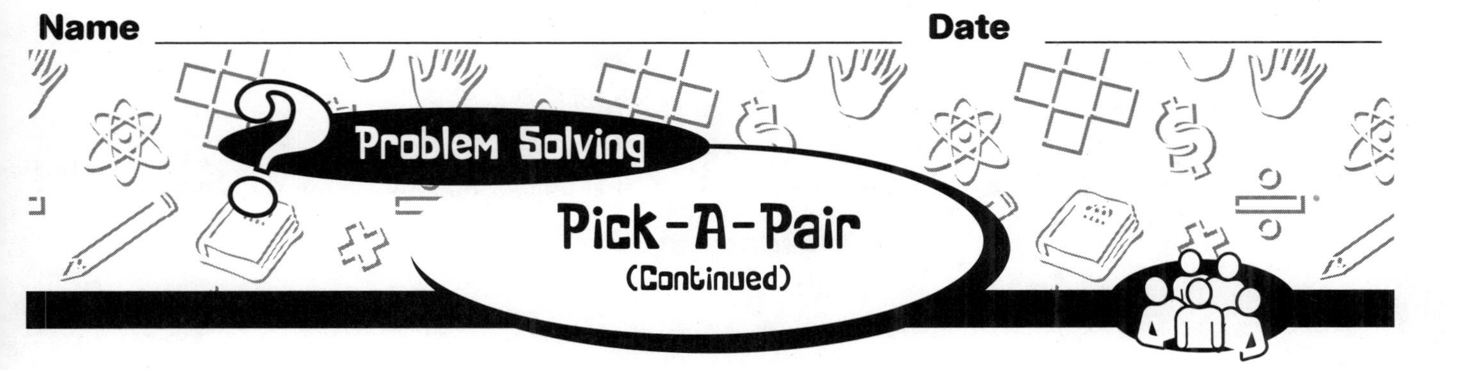

Volume and Distance

Match the equivalent measurements. For example, 2 cups are the same as 1 pint, so match 2 c. with 1 pt. Note: Some measurements appear twice because there are multiple equivalencies.

3 tsp.	1 bushel	1 qt.	10,560 ft.	1 ft.	1 gal.
4 c.	16 oz.	64 oz.	$\frac{1}{2}$ bushel	1 mile	1 rod
8 furlongs	4 qt.	40 yd.	1 qt.	1 Tbsp.	1 pt.
1 c.	3 ft.	2 pecks	1760 yd.	$5\frac{1}{2}$ yd.	1 pt.
12 in.	2 c.	2 mi.	16 Tbsp.	1 c.	1 mi.
4 pecks	1 furlong	32 oz.	1 yd.	8 oz.	$\frac{1}{2}$ gal.

Answers for games:

Animal groups

ants—colony
bees—swarm
clams—bed
elephants—herd
fish—school
geese—flock
gorillas—band
hens—brood
horses—team
kangaroos—troop
kittens—litter
lions—pride
locusts—plague
oxen—yoke
pigs—litter
seals—pod
sheep—flock
wolves—pack

Greek and Roman Gods and Goddesses

Dreams/sleep—Somnus
Earth—Terra
Fire—Vulcan
King of gods—Zeus
Love—Eros
Love—Cupid
Messenger/science/invention—Mercury
Moon—Luna
Queen of gods—Hera
Sea—Poseidon
Spring—Persephone
Sun—Helios
Sun—Apollo
Thunder—Zeus
Underworld/death—Hades
Vengeance—Nemesis
War—Ares
Wisdom—Athena

Volume and Distance

3 tsp. = 1 Tbsp.
16 Tbsp. = 1 c.
2 c. = 1 pt.
4 c. = 1 qt.
4 qt. = 1 gal.
2 pecks = $\frac{1}{2}$ bushel
4 pecks = 1 bushel
8 oz. = 1 c.
16 oz. = 1 pt.
32 oz. = 1 qt.
64 oz. = $\frac{1}{2}$ gal.
12 in. = 1 ft.
3 ft. = 1 yd.
$5\frac{1}{2}$ yd. = 1 rod
40 yd. = 1 furlong
8 furlong = 1 mi.
1760 yd. = 1 mi.
10,560 ft. = 2 mi.

Name ______________________ Date ______________

Here is a challenging game to get your students racing to the chalkboard! Students need to work with their teammates to supply words that use the entire alphabet.

Assign each team its own section of the chalkboard. Each team needs to appoint a "coach" who will keep track of used letters. The coach should write all 26 letters of the alphabet on 1 section of the board before play begins. The object of the game is to be the first team to use all 26 letters of the alphabet in a column of words following these rules:

- No letter can be repeated in a word.
- No word can share a letter with the word above it or below it.

At the teacher's signal, the first person from each team races to the board and writes the word of his choice, being certain to choose a word in which no letter appears more than once. The coach marks off the letters that were used in the first word. At the same time, the first player returns to his seat and the second player comes forward to the board to add a word to her team's word list. She will want to use as many unused letters as possible while following the two rules above. Play continues until one team wins the round by using all 26 letters of the alphabet. Teammates are allowed to discuss possible word choices with each other before going to the board.

Example: Here are two different word lists that use all 26 letters of the alphabet and follow both rules above.

kite	cozy
warm	quilt
soul	bake
zebra	grim
hold	junk
quiet	flax
box	wipe
juicy	sold
gave	hive
upon	
five	

Hint: Use at least 1 "difficult" letter (o, q, z, etc.) in the very first word on your list.

Teachers may add their own variations or restrictions. For example, it could be required that all words contain 4 or more letters, all talking could be banned, etc.

Name ______________________ Date ______________

How quickly can your middle school students find the right way to "sign in"? In this game, players try to be first at figuring out how to add mathematical signs, parentheses, and brackets to correctly solve equations. The only materials needed are the chalkboard, pencils, and scrap paper.

Write this example on the chalkboard before you begin to play to show your class how the game works: 5 4 6 2 = 24

Tell students that by adding any of the 4 operational signs (+ – x ÷) , parentheses and/or brackets, they can make this a correct equation without changing the order of any of the numbers. Here is the solution which will help you to demonstrate: (5 x 4) + (6 – 2) = 24

Now ask students to write 3 equations of their own with 4 numbers to the left of the equal sign. Depending on age and ability, equations could include just 3 numbers, or up to 5 or 6. These are for the students' own reference and will be used if/when they come to the chalkboard. The problems can be drawn on scrap paper and should include the final answer with operational signs, etc. Students should double-check for accuracy.

Choose one student to begin the game. That player goes to the board and writes one of his equations, omitting the signs, parentheses, and brackets. The rest of the class then tries to solve the equation. Anyone who thinks he or she has the answer should raise his or her hand. When recognized by the person who wrote the problem, the solver comes to the board and writes in the missing signs and symbols. If that person is correct, she takes a turn at putting one of her equations on the board. AN IMPORTANT NOTE: Some equations can be correctly solved in more than one way. Any answer that works should be accepted even if it is not identical to the one originally written. Continue playing more rounds as time allows.

Here are more solved equations for your use:

(5 x 6) ÷ (2 + 1) = 10

[(12 ÷ 4) x 5] + 6 = 21

[(9 x 8) – (7 x 6)] ÷ 5 = 6

[(7 + 4) x 5] – 6 = 49

[(3 x 4 x 5) ÷ 6] = 10

[(5 x 10) – (15 + 20)] + 25 = 40

Name ______________________ Date ______________

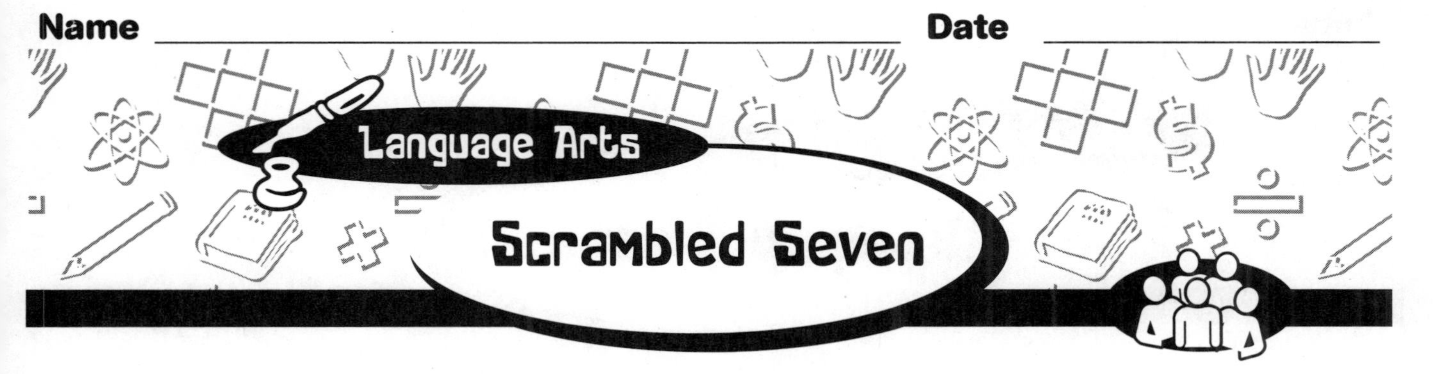

In this game, 2 teams face off to put scrambled sets of letters into sensible words. Each team needs a piece of paper and pencil. A "recorder" should be appointed to write each team's responses.

To play, the teacher writes a group of 7 letters on the board. Team 1 tries to spell 1 word using all 7 letters. At the same time, Team 2 tries to write 10 smaller words using the same group of letters. The first team to reach its goal receives 10 points. For the next round, Team 2 tries to spell one 7-letter word while Team 1 tries to spell 10 smaller words. At the end of playing time, the team with the most points wins.

Example: The letters are: R, A, O, P, M, R, G. Team 2 finds: par, oar, map, mar, gram, ago, rap, ram, rag, prom before Team 1 finds a 7-letter word. (The answer is *program*.) Team 2 receives 10 points; Team 1 receives no points.

Here are twenty 7-letter words that can be scrambled and used for this game:

hamster	stadium	cracker	holiday
tadpole	nothing	trickle	natural
service	deposit	orchard	airport
storage	hogwash	pioneer	protect
lobster	laundry	payment	leather

Name ______________________ Date ______________

Here is a fast-paced A-to-Z game that will keep everybody on their toes! Use it to cover specific content or general knowledge topics. To play this game, you will need a pencil and one copy of the A-to-Z blanks found on the next page for each group of students.

Before the game begins, decide which categories you wish to review and list them on separate slips of paper. Select at least 5 categories. Fold these slips in half and place them in a "hat" or paper bag. For a science unit on human anatomy, for example, you might list: *bones in the skeletal system, organs in the digestive system,* or *names of infectious diseases.* For an advisory period, you might list broader categories such as *European countries, explorers, authors, world rivers,* and *10-letter words.*

Divide the class into groups of 4 to 6 students. Give each group 1 copy of the following page, or instruct students to make a similar form on a piece of plain paper. Ask each group to select a recorder.

Draw 1 slip out of the hat and read it to the class. Give each group 1 minute to list as many answers as possible for that category. The recorder for each group must write the answers next to each beginning letter as the other players call them out. During this minute, the recorder needs to remind his team which letters are crossed out (already used) and which letters still need to be used in starting a word.

After 1 minute, move on to a new category, keeping the A-to-Z page from the first round. Obviously, the more categories you use, the harder it is for students to think of answers, especially for infrequently used letters such as J, Q, and Z.

Continue in this manner until 1 team has filled in all 26 letters or until you have called out 5 categories. After 5 categories, stop the game and ask teams to count up the number of letters used. Quickly check the answers supplied by each team as each recorder reads them aloud. The winning team is either the one to complete all 26 letters or the one with the most correct answers after 5 rounds.

Begin a new game with 5 new categories as time allows.

Example:
First category: *bones in the skeletal system*
Answers for Group 1: *clavicle, femur, fibula* (cannot use this because **f** has already been used), *humerus, mandible, patella, ribs, sternum*
Second category: *organs in the digestive system*
Answers for Group 1: *esophagus, liver, stomach* (cannot use because **s** was used in previous category), *large intestine* (cannot use because **l** has already been used in *liver*, but group might change this to *intestine* since letter *i* has not been used) .

Name ______________________________ Date ______________

Problem Solving

Category Cross-Out
(Continued)

A-to-Z Chart

A	______	N	______
B	______	O	______
C	______	P	______
D	______	Q	______
E	______	R	______
F	______	S	______
G	______	T	______
H	______	U	______
I	______	V	______
J	______	W	______
K	______	X	______
L	______	Y	______
M	______	Z	______

Name ____________________ Date ____________

On this page and the next, you will find 2 fun games to review important people in history. Keep these games in mind when your students read the biographies of inventors, scientists, authors, explorers and others.

Famous Figures 1—Hidden Identities

In this game, students will try to remember key facts about important people or characters from the past or present. Use this game to review historical figures, current world leaders, athletes, fictional characters from well-known literary works, and more. First, decide on a list of famous names, so that there is 1 name for each student. Write each name on a separate sheet of paper.

Ask students to line up facing a classroom wall so that they cannot see the names on the pieces of paper. Tape a name to the back of each student with masking tape.

Instruct students to begin moving carefully around the room, reading the names on the backs of classmates and asking questions to try to find their own identities.

Students may ask questions such as:
"Am I a real person?"
"Am I living now?"
"Am I an American?"
"Am I known for playing sports?"

Each question may only be answered with a "yes" or "no." To keep students moving around, tell them they may only ask 2 questions of the same person at a time.

When a player thinks he or she knows the identity, that player may ask another player, "Am I Ronald Reagan?" If the answer is "yes," the name is removed from his back. He may still play to answer questions for others. Continue playing the game as long as time permits or until each student has found his own famous name.

Name ______________________________ Date ______________

Famous Figures—Signatures

How many signatures of famous people of the past or present can your students collect? Play this game to review important facts about important people from around the world, and let your students help you to write the game!

After studying famous people (scientists, authors, explorers, inventors, athletes, musicians, etc.), assign one special person for each student to research. While you may require extensive reports during your unit of this study, for this game each student only needs a few key facts. Ask each student to write down 3 important, distinctive facts about a famous person. These facts should then be handed to the teacher.

The teacher needs to make 1 master list using information from student research. You may choose to use 1, 2, or all 3 of the facts that each student turned in. Copy these facts into a single document, mixing up the facts and leaving space between them for "signatures."

When you are ready to play the game, ask each student to wear an easy-to-read label that bears the name of the person he has researched. Distribute a copy of your "master list" to each player. Upon your signal, each student is to circulate around the room trying to obtain "signatures" of people who are described on the master list. Students may only ask specific questions, not general ones such as, "Is there any fact on my list which you can autograph?"

For example, suppose that Beth was assigned to research Harriet Beecher Stowe. For her 3 facts she wrote:

1) This person was born in Connecticut in 1811.
2) She attended Connecticut Female Seminary and married a theology professor.
3) This person authored *Uncle Tom's Cabin.*

Beth's teacher compiles 2 of these facts (1 and 3) with 2 facts from every other student in the class. Sally reads the master list and thinks that Beth's character, Ms. Stowe, is the author of *Uncle Tom's Cabin.* So Sally asks, "Beth, can you sign my page as the author of *Uncle Tom's Cabin*?" Beth, of course, agrees and signs the name of her character.

The first player to collect signatures for every fact is the winner. Or, the winner is the person who collects the most signatures before time runs out.

Name ______________________ Date ______________

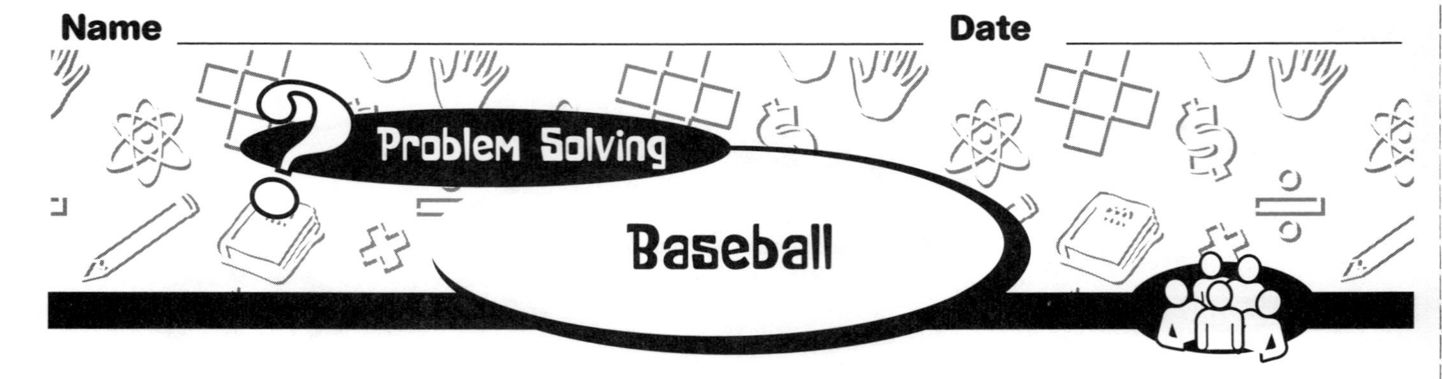

Baseball

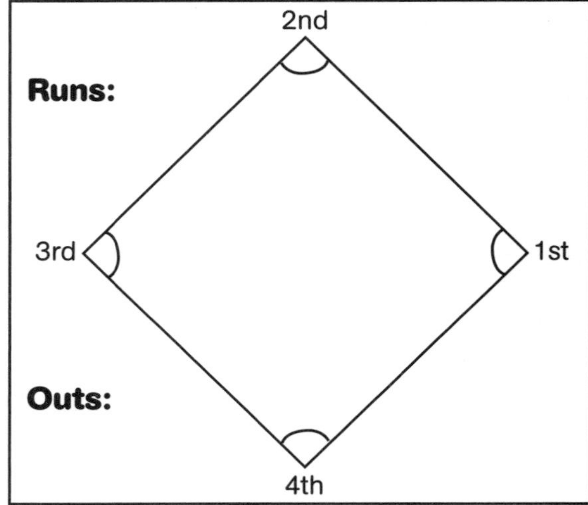

Batter up! Get your students into the swing of learning with this traditional game. First write questions appropriate for your current unit of study. Write questions that have short, specific answers. Divide your questions by difficulty into 4 categories: single, double, triple, and home run. (Singles are the easiest questions, home runs are the most difficult.) You may even wish to have students help write questions as part of the unit review process. For your convenience, a few questions on assorted middle-school topics are included on the next page. You may use these to begin your own list.*

To play, divide the class into 2 teams and decide which team will bat first. Draw a simple baseball diamond on the chalkboard that contains all the bases. Appoint a scorekeeper for each team. (This student may also take his turn at bat.)

The first batter on Team 1 selects the level of difficulty for the question he will attempt to answer. If he answers correctly, he gets a runner on base. For example, suppose that Tony is first and he chooses a single. If he answers correctly, his scorekeeper draws an **X** on first base. Suppose that Peggy is the next batter and she selects a triple. If she answers correctly, Tony's runner advances to home plate and scores a run for Team 1. Peggy's **X** goes to third base. If Peggy answers incorrectly, Tony's **X** stays on first base, and Team 1 has its first out. The scorekeeper is responsible for tallying outs and runs for his team.

Continue playing until Team 1 has committed 3 outs. At that point, the team's turn is over and Team 2 comes up to bat. Continue playing so that each team has an equal number of turns at bat. The team with the most runs wins.

*On the next page, you will find 6 questions listed for each category. You may want to use some or all of these for your class, or you may simply use these for ideas. You will need many more questions than this, especially if you want to play baseball for an entire class period.

Name ______________________ Date ____________

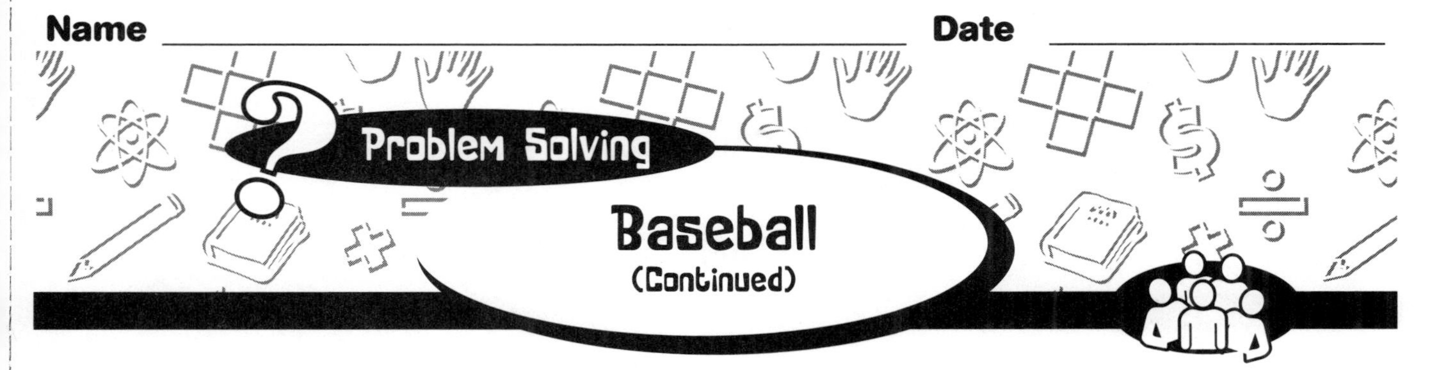

Baseball Sample Questions:

Singles:
1. How many yards are in a mile? (1,760)
2. Who was the third U.S. President? (Thomas Jefferson)
3. Spell the word *receive.*
4. What element is symbolized by the letter H? (hydrogen)
5. What is the capital of Illinois? (Springfield)
6. List all the factors of 12. (1, 2, 3, 4, 6, 12)

Doubles:
1. What is the greatest common factor of 32, 60, and 20? (4)
2. Put these cities in order from north to south: Richmond, VA; Minneapolis, MN; Indianapolis, IN. (Minneapolis, Indianapolis, Richmond)
3. Start with the word *plates.* Rearrange the same letters to spell 2 more words. (Any two of these: petals, staple, pastel)
4. Who invented bifocal lenses in 1784? (Benjamin Franklin)
5. What is the name for a story someone writes about his/her own life? (autobiography)
6. What is the capital of Australia? (Canberra)

Triples:
1. Name the two men who served as vice-president while Richard Nixon was President. (Spiro Agnew and Gerald Ford)
2. How many cups are there in a gallon? (16)
3. Who wrote *Alice's Adventures in Wonderland*? (Lewis Carroll)
4. During which years was the United States active in World War II? (1941–45)
5. Spell the word *embarrass.*
6. What amendment to the U.S. Constitution abolished slavery? (13th Amendment)

Home Runs:
1. Name the 4 countries that make up the United Kingdom. (England, Scotland, Wales, Northern Ireland)
2. Multiply the square root of 144 by the cube root of 27. Add 6 and divide by 7. What is the answer? (6)
3. What was the first state in the U.S. to give women the right to vote? (Wyoming)
4. Who is the only U.S. President to serve non-consecutive terms? (Cleveland)
5. Name the 5 Great Lakes in order from largest to smallest. (Superior, Huron, Michigan, Erie, and Ontario)
6. What is the name and location of the longest bone in the human body? (femur, thigh)

Name ______________________ Date ____________

If you have recently studied the Gettysburg Address, the Preamble to the U.S. Constitution, or some other significant document from history, here's a fun way to review it.* You may choose to have students work on their own, or you may assign them to work with a partner. Each player (or pair) needs paper and pencil.

Tell the players that you are going to read the Preamble to the U.S. Constitution (or Lincoln's Gettysburg Address, etc.), but that you will occasionally leave out words. The players are to write down all the missing words. (If working in pairs, partners will have to discuss the missing words very quickly and quietly.) Explain that you will always tell them how many words you are omitting.

Then slowly read the Preamble or Lincoln's address. A sample reading of both are included here, with omitted words in parentheses. As you read, pause at each blank to allow the students to write the missing words on their papers. Remember to tell everyone how many words are missing. Have players trade papers. Then read through the entire Preamble or Address aloud, including the words that were left out before. The player or team with the most correct words is the winner.

*You could also review patriotic songs or excerpts from literature that you have asked students to memorize.

****

Preamble to the United States Constitution:

We, the People of the (United States), in order to form a more (perfect) Union, establish (justice), insure (domestic tranquility), provide for the common (defense), promote the general welfare, and (secure) the blessings of (liberty) to ourselves and our (posterity), do ordain and (establish) this Constitution for the United States of America.

Name ______________________ Date ______________

Lincoln's Gettysburg Address

Four score and seven years ago our fathers brought forth, upon this (continent), a new nation, conceived in (Liberty), and dedicated to the proposition that all men are created (equal).

Now we are engaged in a (great civil war), testing whether that nation, or any nation so conceived, and so dedicated, can long (endure). We are met on a great battlefield of that (war). We have come to dedicate a portion of it as a (final resting place) for those who here gave their lives that that nation might (live). It is altogether fitting and (proper) that we should do this.

But in a larger sense we cannot (dedicate)—we cannot consecrate—we cannot hallow—this ground. The brave men, (living and dead), who struggled here, have consecrated it far above our poor (power) to add or detract. The world will little note, nor long (remember) what we say here, but it can never (forget) what they (did) here. It is for us, the living, rather to be dedicated here to the (unfinished work) which they have, thus far, so nobly (carried on). It is rather for us to be here dedicated to the (great task) remaining before us—that from these honored dead we take increased devotion to that cause for which they gave the last (full measure) of devotion—that we here highly resolve that these dead shall not have (died in vain); that this nation shall have a new birth of (freedom); and that this government of the people, by the people, for the people, shall not perish from the (earth).

Your students will really have to listen and concentrate to successfully complete this activity. Students will need some basic knowledge of U.S. geography, good listening skills, a blank piece of paper, and a pencil. Students may either work individually or in pairs. Be ready to reward a prize to anyone who comes up with the right answer.

Read these instructions aloud to the entire class:

1. On the left-hand side of your paper, about half way down the page, write *Denver.*
2. To the right of Denver write *Chicago.*
3. If the population of Chicago is larger than that of Denver, write *Little Rock* under Chicago.
4. If it is farther from Chicago to Denver than it is from Little Rock to Dallas, cross out Little Rock and write *Detroit* to the right of Chicago.
5. If Boston is not larger than Detroit, write *Boston* above Detroit.
6. If Des Moines is north of New Orleans, write *Tampa* under Detroit.
7. Do not cross out Boston unless it is not in New Jersey.
8. If Milwaukee is west of Detroit, write the state in which Milwaukee is located above Chicago.
9. If Chicago is the capital of Illinois, cross out Detroit.
10. Write *Phoenix* under Denver unless it is north of Denver, in which case you should write Phoenix above Denver.
11. If 3 cities on your paper are west of the Mississippi River, circle those cities. If there are not 3 cities west of the Mississippi River, don't circle any of them.
12. Write Miami under Tampa only if Tampa is in Georgia.

Answer:

	Wisconsin	~~Boston~~
Denver	Chicago	Detroit
Phoenix	~~Little Rock~~	Tampa

Name ____________________ **Date** ____________

As with the previous page, your students will have to listen and concentrate to complete this activity successfully. Students will need some basic knowledge of world geography, good listening skills, a blank piece of paper, and a pencil. Once again, you may wish to have students complete this activity individually or in pairs.

Read these instructions aloud to the entire class:

1. If Australia is south of Asia, write *Asia* in the center of your paper.
2. If the Pacific Ocean lies between North America and Europe, underline Asia.
3. If the Equator runs through both South America and Africa, write Africa to the left of Asia.
4. If Italy is part of Europe, write *Europe* on your page above Africa.
5. If Brazil is in North America, write *North America* above Europe.
6. If India is part of Asia, write *India* under Asia.
7. If Australia is not both a country and a continent, write *Australia* at the bottom center of your page.
8. If the Tropic of Cancer is north of the Equator, draw a line across the top of your paper. If it's south of the Equator, draw a line across the bottom of your paper.
9. If the Panama Canal runs between Central America and South America, write the initials, *C.A.S.A.* near the bottom left comer of your page.
10. If Japan is not part of Asia, cross out Asia.
11. If Russia is part of both Europe and Asia, circle Europe and Asia.
12. If the Sahara Desert is not in India, cross out India.

Answer:

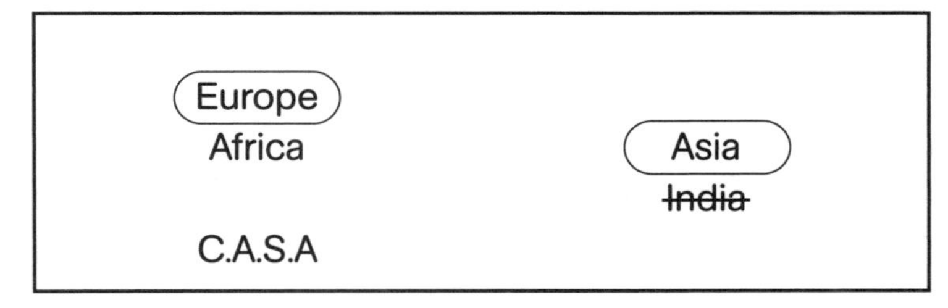

Name ______________________ Date ______________

Random Risks

This game combines luck with mathematical skill. Risk takers might win or they might lose! Allow your entire class to compete in this fun game that emphasizes place value and computational skills. Students are presented with problem formats, or patterns, and are asked to place random digits in those patterns with a goal of generating the highest or lowest possible sum, difference, or product.

Before the game begins, prepare 10 cards numbered 0 to 9. Place all 10 cards in a paper bag or container.

When you are ready to play, draw 1 of the patterns from the next page on the chalkboard. Instruct students to draw the same pattern on a piece of paper at their desks. (Scrap paper works fine for this game.) Decide if you are playing to find the highest answer or the lowest before numbers are drawn.

Next, walk around the classroom, selecting a student to take a turn at drawing a number out of the bag. Each time a digit is drawn, every student must write that digit in some position in their problem. Do not replace the number that has been drawn. Continue asking students to draw numbers out of the bag until enough numbers have been drawn to complete the problem.

When students have completed writing their problems, they should then calculate the sum, difference, or product. Ask students to share their answers. In a short amount of time, you should be able to tell who the winners are. Then review the pattern and the numbers drawn with the class and discuss if the highest (or lowest) possible answer was generated.

Play more rounds as time allows. It is suggested that you use each pattern a few times with both high and low answers before moving on to another format.

Example: Using this pattern, students are asked to find the highest sum.

$$\begin{array}{r} \square\square\square \\ +\ \square\square \\ \hline \end{array}$$

In order, the numbers drawn were 6, 3, 4, 7, and 1.

Brandon's final problem was $\begin{array}{r} 163 \\ +\ 74 \\ \hline 237 \end{array}$ He was obviously hoping the 8 or 9 would be drawn as the last digit, rather than 1 and had saved the most "valuable" spot for the last digit.	Nate's final problem was $\begin{array}{r} 671 \\ +\ 43 \\ \hline 714 \end{array}$ Nate didn't take much risk but he clearly beat Brandon.

Neither of them arrived at the problem with the highest possible sum which was:
761 + 43 = 804 (or 741 + 63, 763 + 41, 743 + 61, etc.)

Name ______________________ Date ____________

Here are several different patterns to use for mathematical problems when playing "Random Risks." You may decide to try more patterns of your own as well. Remember: Ask students to aim for the highest and lowest answers for each one. You may want to allow students to use calculators for this one.

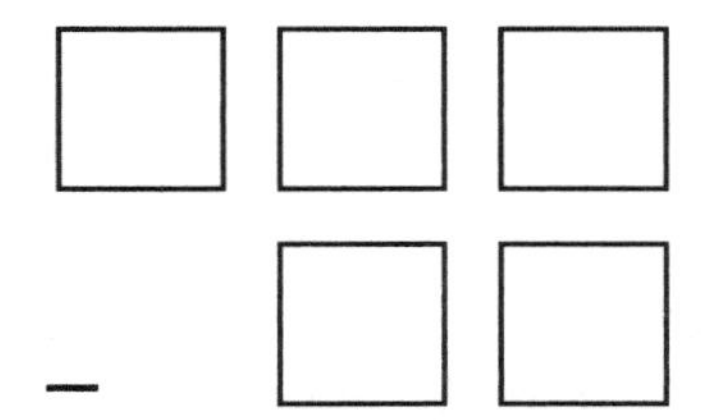

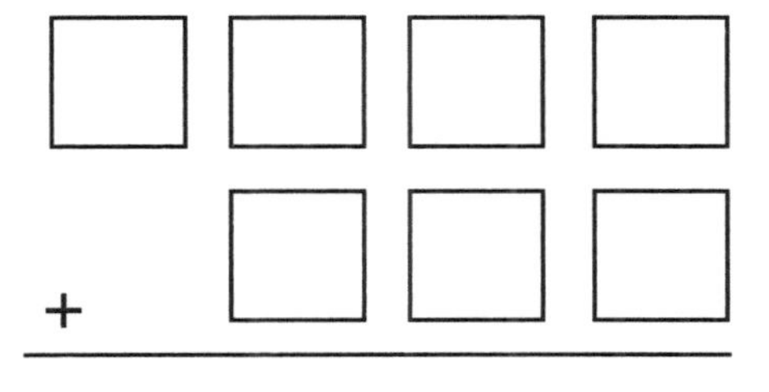

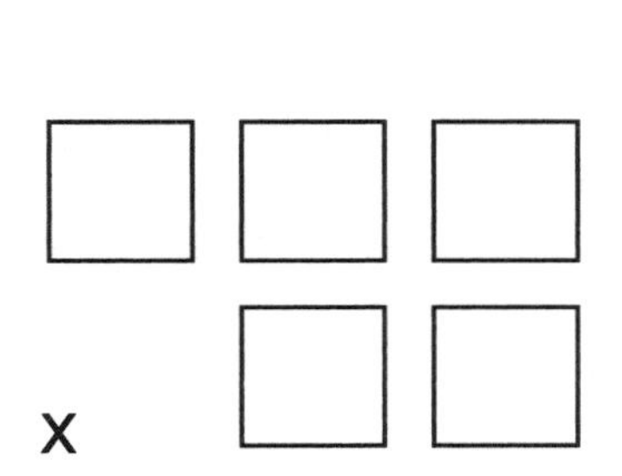

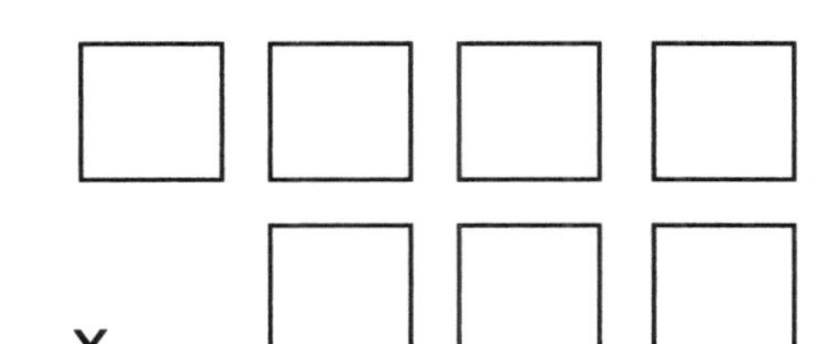

These problems use fractions:

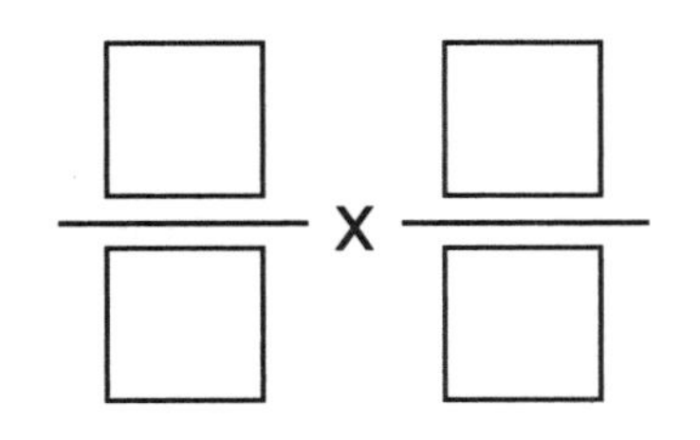

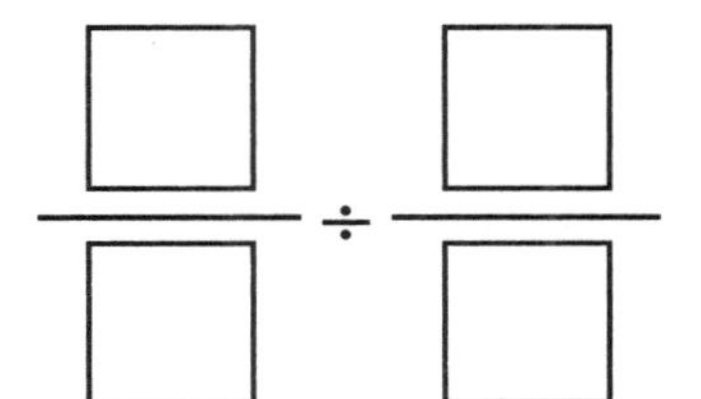

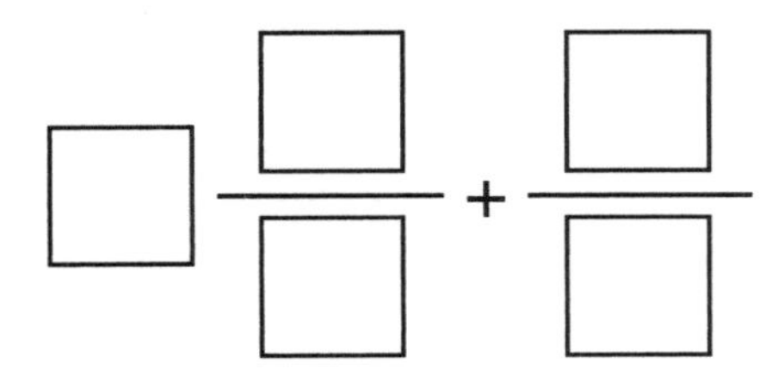

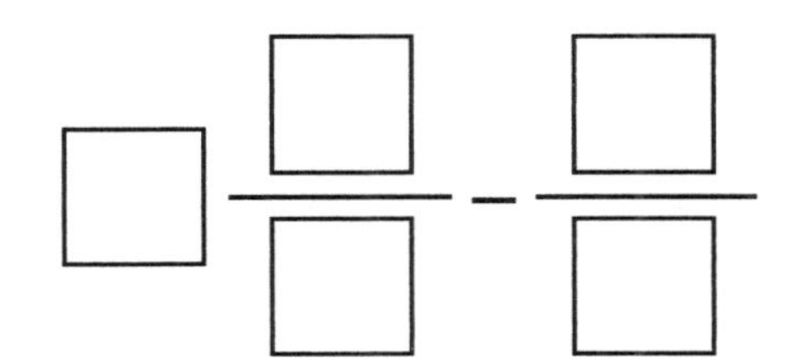

Name ______________________ Date ____________

Here are 3 different games and activities that use proverbs, those short bits of sage advice. These activities are arranged from easiest to most difficult. A list of proverbs is provided on the following page for your reference.

Proverbial Wisdom
Proverbs are said to be wise sayings. A person's wisdom, then, could be judged by the number of proverbs he knows. Give your students 10 minutes to write down all the proverbs they can think of. The one with the longest list is the winner (or maybe the wisest).

Proverbial Showdown
Divide your class into 2 teams of equal number and have them sit or stand so they are facing each other. The first person on Team 1 goes over to Team 2, points at a member of the team and starts counting. This player must give a proverb before the pointer can count to 20. If this player succeeds, he then goes over to the first team and points out a player, who in turn must quote a proverb while he counts to 20. If a player cannot respond with a proverb before the count of 20, he must go over to the opposing team as a captive, and the player who pointed him out has a chance at another player. A proverb given once may not be repeated. The longer the game continues, the more difficult it is for players to state a proverb that has not already been used. The game may continue until one side has captured all of the players of the other side.

Proverbial Questions
One student is sent out of the room, and while she is gone, the rest of the students decide on a proverb. When the first player returns, she must determine what the proverb is by asking questions. The first person questioned must include in his answer the first word of the proverb, the second one questioned must include in his answer the second word of the proverb, the third one questioned must include the third word in the proverb and so on. The questioner should be told how many words are in the proverb so that she will know how many questions to ask. If the questioner discovers the proverb, the one from whom she received her clue in identifying it must go out of the room for the next round.

Example: The class selects, *Practice makes perfect.* Lisa comes into the room and is told the class has chosen a 3-word proverb. Lisa needs to ask only 3 questions. First she asks Aaron, "How is your day going?" Aaron answers, "My day is going well, except for the fact that we had to *practice* somersaults all through gym class." Lisa then asks Phoebe, "What did you have for lunch?" Phoebe replies, "My mom *makes* the best tuna sandwiches. That's what I ate." Lisa finally asks Jim, "What's your favorite color?" He answers, "A *perfect* shade of sky blue is my favorite color." Lisa must now think through all of the clues to determine what the proverb might be. She decides that Jim's use of the word *perfect* was a bit unusual so that must be the hidden word in his answer. She then decides the answer must be *practice makes perfect.* Jim then leaves the room, and the class picks a new proverb.

Name ______________________ Date ______________

This list of proverbs will be a useful reference for the activities.

1. A friend in need is a friend indeed.
2. A miss is as good as a mile.
3. Actions speak louder than words.
4. Don't put the cart before the horse.
5. Two's company; three's a crowd.
6. Too many cooks spoil the broth.
7. Haste makes waste.
8. A stitch in time saves nine.
9. Two heads are better than one.
10. Make hay while the sun shines.
11. If the shoe fits, wear it.
12. A fool and his money are soon parted.
13. Birds of a feather flock together.
14. Misery loves company.
15. Practice makes perfect.
16. Still water runs deep.
17. A word to the wise is sufficient.
18. Laugh and the world laughs with you.
19. Every cloud has a silver lining.
20. Never count your chickens before they are hatched.
21. No news is good news.
22. Out of sight, out of mind.
23. Better late than never.
24. Variety is the spice of life.
25. Honesty is the best policy.
26. Many hands make light work.
27. Never put off until tomorrow what you can do today.
28. The early bird catches the worm.
29. The pen is mightier than the sword.
30. Nothing ventured, nothing gained.
31. Never look a gift horse in the mouth.
32. One good turn deserves another.
33. Save the pennies and the dollars will take care of themselves.
34. If at first you don't succeed, try, try, again.
35. A man's house is his castle.

Name ______________________ Date ____________

Can your students list the capitals and major cities of the United States? If they can, they're ready for a game of Citywide Bingo! Each student will need a copy of the empty grid on the next page (or a sheet of unlined paper which they should divide into a 5 x 5 grid of boxes, as shown) and a supply of colored squares to use as markers.

Instruct each player to fill in her grid with her choice of states. By excluding the "free" space, there are only 24 boxes in which to write the names of states, so the players will have plenty from which to choose.

Next, let the fun begin as you choose from one of these variations of "Citywide Bingo"!

Capitals
In random order, call out the capital cities of the 50 states in the U.S. If a student has the name of the state for which the city serves as state capital on her card, she covers that state with a marker. The first player to cover 5 squares in a row—vertically, horizontally, or diagonally—calls out, "Bingo!" She then reads back to the teacher the names of the states she has covered. If all answers are correct, she is the winner for that round. Play several more rounds as time allows. Encourage students to replace the names of some states between rounds.

Major Cities
In random order, call out the major cities (that are not capitals) of several states. For example, you might call out, "Dallas and Fort Worth," for the state of Texas. If a student has the name of the state in which the cities belong on his card, he covers that state with a marker. Play continues as described above. A U.S. map or atlas will be helpful to you.

State Mottos or Nicknames
It is always fun to review state nicknames. For example, call out "The Keystone State" for Pennsylvania.

World Cities
For this game, have students make new bingo cards, filling in the names of 24 countries. You might choose to emphasize 2 continents at a time for this game. Randomly call out the capitals and/or major cities of countries around the world as players mark their cards as described above.

Name ______________________ Date ______________

Citywide Bingo!
(Continued)

		FREE		

Here is an educational twist to an old favorite. Draw this diagram on the chalkboard or on an overhead transparency. (You may want to make it a permanent transparency, and then add Xs and Os with a wipe-off marker.) Prepare several questions ahead of time, about 9 questions for each round that you intend to play. The questions can review material from any content area, or they can cover general knowledge.

1	2	3
4	5	6
7	8	9

Divide your class into 2 teams, and decide which team starts. Read the first question aloud to Team 1. If that team answers correctly, they choose in which square they will place an **X**. Then it is Team 2's turn to answer the next question. If they answer correctly, they choose in which square they will place an **O**. (Having the squares numbered simplifies communication.) When a question is not answered correctly, no **X** or **O** is given on that round.

Each round ends when a team scores 3 marks in a row, either vertically, horizontally, or diagonally. When starting the next round, let the "losers" go first.

Variation: If Team 1 is unable to answer their question correctly, Team 2 gets a chance to "steal" an extra box. If Team 2 supplies the right answer, they are allowed to place an **O** on the tic-tac-toe board. On the next round, the question goes first to Team 2, as it would if Team 1 had answered correctly.

Name ____________________ Date ____________

Speed Art

Here's a lively game in which your students can review vocabulary words, historical events, literary characters, and more. You will need to divide your class into groups of 4 or 5 students each. Each team will need its own sketch paper (plain white paper, the backs of unused worksheets, etc.), a pencil or marker, and a list of words/names. Each team should also decide among themselves who will draw first, second, third, and so on.

Before the game begins, decide which words you want to use. For example, you may wish to review spelling words from last month, or the new terms in the current chapter of the science text. Tell students what general topic you are using before starting the game. Make a list of 10 words or names for each group of students. Each list should be different, although it is okay to use some terms on more than one list. Cut apart each team list into 10 separate strips of paper. Fold these in half and place in an envelope, paper cup, or bag. Give one set of 10 words to each team.

On your signal, the first artist for each team reaches into the envelope and draws out a slip of paper. He reads it to himself but is not allowed to show it to his teammates. As quickly as possible, the artist draws a picture for the rest of his team to illustrate the meaning of the word. The teammates try to guess the word. When someone calls out the correct answer, the first artist passes his marker to the next artist. Play continues until a team has correctly identified all 10 words. TIP: Since more than 1 team may have some of the same words, students should try to work rather quietly to avoid giving hints to their opponents.

Drawing rules:
Clarify the rules ahead of time with the entire class. Do not allow students to write words or letters when drawing. You can decide whether or not to allow numbers. Also, remind students that they are to draw, rather than act out, the words.

Drawing ideas:

- For vocabulary words, students should try to draw a picture that relates to the word. For example, if the vocabulary word was *pompous*, the student might draw a large king with a big crown and tiny stick people at his feet.
- For historical events, students could draw symbols associated with special dates. If the event were the Battle of Gettysburg, someone might draw horses, cannons, soldiers, and a map of Pennsylvania.
- For literary figures, students will want to draw pictures that remind their classmates about the book in which the character is found. For example, if the character was Tiny Tim from *A Christmas Carol,* the artist might draw a Christmas tree and a pair of crutches.

Variation: For a shorter game, use lists of only 5 words.

Name ______________________ Date ____________

In most spelling games, the object is to complete words correctly. But in this game, the object is to not complete a word at all!

Divide your students into two teams for this fun-filled spelling and vocabulary game. Students may be divided in any way you choose and arranged in any order on each team. The first student on Team 1 calls out a letter. The first student on Team 2 adds a letter to the first that could be used in spelling a correct word. Then the second student on Team 1 adds a third letter. Play moves back and forth between the 2 teams, with a different person on each team adding a letter as play goes on.

The catch is to NOT complete a word. If the letter a player adds is the final letter in an actual word, the other team is awarded a point. If a player cannot think of a letter to add to the chain of letters, the opposing team also gets a point. The team with the most points at the end of playing time is the winner.

Note: The player must always have a word in mind when adding letters. If anyone adds to the letter chain without having a definite word in mind he is open to be challenged. If he cannot name a word when challenged, the opposing team is awarded a point and a new round is started.

Here is how a sample game might be played:

The first player on Team 1 calls out the letter E. The first player on Team 2 calls out the letter G, with the word *egg* in mind. The next player on Team I is not about to get caught completing the word *egg*. She remembers that she has before heard the word *egret* which is a kind of bird. So she adds the letter R. The next player on Team 2 is stumped and cannot add a letter. So Team 1 is awarded 1 point.

Suppose a new round is started. Team 2 begins with the letter U. The player from Team 1 thinks of the word *upper* and adds P. But the P completes the word *up*, so Team 2 picks up a point.

Name ______________________ Date ______________

Here is a simple, humorous memory game for the whole class that requires no material or advance preparation.

The first player begins by saying, "one acrobatic antelope," or another similar phrase that begins with the word *one*, followed by an adjective and noun that begin with the letter **a**.

The second player repeats the first phrase and then adds an additional phrase, which must begin with the word *two*, followed by an adjective and a noun that begin with **b**.

The third player must repeat the *one* and *two* phrases, and then add a new phrase that begins with *three* and continues on with the alphabet.

Play continues until some players can no longer remember all the phrases and must drop out. The last one to remember all the phrases and add a new phrase is the winner.

Here are more sample phrases:
- one awful anteater
- two bald buffaloes
- three crooked chimneys
- four daring dinosaurs
- five edible eggplants

If all the letters of the alphabet have been used and players are still in the game, begin the alphabet over again. For example, you might say *twenty-seven artistic alligators, twenty-eight bruised badgers,* etc.

Name ______________________ Date ______________

Here is a quick game for when you have just a few minutes to fill, and you want to keep middle school minds working on something positive. So that students can work on mental calculations and good listening skills, do not allow them to use paper and pencil. Ask students to raise their hands as soon as they know the answer. Award 1 point to the first person with the right answer. There is a wide range of difficulty purposely included here to encourage the weaker students and to also challenge the stronger ones.

Variation 1: Divide the class into 2 teams and keep score for each team. Tell students to remember which team they are on so that you can quickly regroup when you've only a few minutes to play. Keep a running tally of points over several days.
Variation 2: Let students compete individually. Players are responsible for keeping their own score.

Questions to use:

1. In one middle school there are 169 boys and 211 girls. How many students are there altogether? (380)

2. There are 24 hours in a day and 60 minutes in an hour. How many minutes are there in 1 day? (1,440)

3. How many cookies are there in 9 dozen? (108)

4. How many yards are there in 66 feet? (22)

5. What is the value of XXIV in Roman numerals? (24)

6. One mile equals 8 furlongs. How many furlongs are there in $9\frac{1}{2}$ miles? (76)

7. In decimal numbers, what does one tenth (0.1) plus one hundredth (0.01) equal? (eleven hundredths or 0.11)

8. Gasoline is $1.50 a gallon. What is the price of 6 gallons? ($9.00)

9. Sales tax is 6%. How much tax will I pay on a purchase of $200? ($12)

10. In one square mile, there are 640 acres. How many acres are there in 3 square miles? (1,920)

11. What is 50% of 320? (160)

12. What percentage of 200 is 50? (25%)

Name ______________________ Date ____________

13. How many days are in the last 2 months of the year? (61)

14. The thermometer shows 40° F in the morning and -15°F at night. How many degrees did the thermometer fall? (55°)

15. If one pair of shoelaces costs $1.05, what will be the price of 5 pairs of shoelaces? ($5.25)

16. Sara starts work at 9 A.M. and works for $7\frac{1}{2}$ hours. She also has a l-hour lunch break. At what time does Sara finish working? (5:30)

17. What is the value of MCM in Roman numerals? (1,900)

18. What is the area of a 5-inch square? (25 square inches)

19. I started the day with 6 dozen eggs, but I broke 14 of them. How many eggs do I have now? (58 eggs or two less than 5 dozen)

20. The rat population of a certain town was 10,000. A rodent disease killed $\frac{2}{5}$ of them. How many are left? (6,000)

21. How many 9-oz. bags of candy can be filled from a 9-lb. sack? (16)

22. What is the value of 2 quarters, 2 dimes, 2 nickels, plus 2 pennies? (82¢)

23. I started the day with $5.00, but I bought 2 comic books, each of which cost $1.49. How much money do I have left? ($2.02)

24. What is the square of 7? (49)

25. Ten feet and 8 inches equals how many inches? (128)

26. What is the remainder when 60 is divided by 8? (4)

27. A motorcycle driver travels at a constant speed of 60 m.p.h. He leaves at noon and drives 150 miles to his hometown. What time does he arrive? (2:30 P.M.)

28. Two numbers have a difference of 5. Their sum is 9. What are the numbers? (2, 7)

29. What is $\frac{1}{3}$ of 48? (16)

30. What is the value of 10 to the fourth power (10^4) ? (10,000)

Parts Smarts

This activity will test your students' abilities in identifying how words are used as different parts of speech. First, divide your class into two teams, and make the word list on this page available to all students. You could write the words on the chalkboard or the overhead projector, or reproduce this page for students.

To begin the game, Team 1 selects any word from the list below, and decides how to use it. Team 1 composes a sentence, reads it aloud and identifies how the listed word is used. Team 2 then must use the same word as a different part of speech. Team 1 may also try to form a sentence for some words in which the word can be used as a third part-of-speech. For the second round, Team 2 goes first. Play ends when time runs out. (Additional words may be added if necessary.) The winning team is the one with the most points.

Each team receives 1 point for correctly using a word and identifying the part of speech that it plays in their sentence. Each team receives an additional point if their opponents are unable to use the same word as a different part of speech.

Example: Team 1 selects *record* and reads the sentence: *My uncle set a record in pole vaulting*. Team 1 announces they have used the word as a noun. Team 2 might then use *record* in this sentence: *We want to record the daily temperature for the month of May.* They correctly state that they have used *record* as a verb. Each team receives 1 point.

Word list:

bank	tee	insert	base	bear	combat
clown	order	wall	weather	level	weed
light	parrot	water	patch	tense	beef
grade	feed	pool	power	turn	style
pump	front	encounter	count	blow	punch
mess	link	puncture	guide	wrinkle	snake
solid	nest	need	draft	deck	air

Name ______________________ Date ______________

Here is a great way to practice all those vocabulary words, geography terms, and science definitions. Each student will create his own game board on his desk. Then he will try to be the first one to Score Four!

Each student will need at least 16 index cards (or slips of paper about the same size), a pencil, and a master list of vocabulary words. The list may be found in a textbook, the chalkboard, or on a worksheet that you supply. The master list should contain 20 or more words.

Before the game begins, each player needs to choose 16 words or terms from the master list. Each player should write the term on the front of the card and its definition on the back. Then that player arranges the cards in a 4 x 4 grid on his or her desk as shown:

benign	terrace	delirious	revive
crude	cathedral	publicity	adorn
deprive	conscious	principle	patriarch
impeded	enterprise	melancholy	conceit

When everyone is ready, the teacher reads 1 definition. All players that have the matching word on their desks may call out the word and remove it from their grids. The player who calls out the word first (as recognized by the teacher) chooses the next definition. He reads it aloud from one of his own cards and then is allowed to remove that card from his desk. Again, the teacher decides who was the first to call out the word, and that player announces the next definition. Play continues until 1 player has removed 4 cards in a row—horizontally, vertically, or diagonally. That player stands up and calls out, "Score Four."

Play more rounds as time allows. For each new round, students may rearrange their words or substitute new words.

Variations: Practice states or countries/capitals, inventors/inventions or other lists this way.

Declare war on mathematical mistakes with this fun card game! Players in this game will try to pull the knot on a “rope” to their own finish line, but all the pulling is done right in the classroom. There’s lots of fun without rope burns and dirty clothes!

You will need an overhead projector, a copy of the cards shown on the next page, an overhead transparency, and a piece of yam tied with a big knot in the middle. First duplicate and cut apart the game cards shown on the next page. Shuffle them and place them face down next to the overhead projector. Then prepare the transparency by drawing a game board like the one shown here:

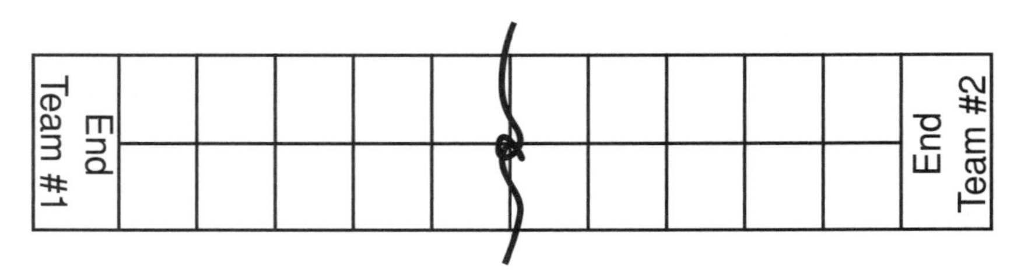

Lay the knotted piece of yarn on top of the game board as shown. Divide the class into 2 teams. To make the competition more fun, you might encourage teams to come up with a special sports name.

To play the game, ask the first player from Team 1 to draw a card, read the sentence on it, and decide if the answer is true (correct) or false (incorrect). If the player gives the correct answer, move the knot 1 mark closer to Team 1’s goal. If his answer is incorrect, move the knot 1 mark closer to Team 2’s goal. Take turns between the members of each team until 1 team moves the knot past its fifth marker. The first team to move the knot past its fifth marker is the winner. Play additional rounds as time allows, preferably until all students have had at least 1 turn.

Here are answers for the cards that follow on page 119. Of course, you may choose to make your own cards to fit the subject area you want to review.

1. true 2. true 3. false 4. true 5. true
6. false 7. false 8. false 9. true 10. false
11. false 12. true 13. true 14. true 15. false
16. false 17. false 18. true 19. true 20. false
21. true 22. false 23. false 24. true 25. false
26. true 27. false 28. true 29. false 30. true

Name ______________________________ Date ________________

1. A prime number is one that has only 2 factors; 1 and itself.	2. Composite numbers always have at least 3 factors.	3. There are 5 prime numbers between 1 and 10.	4. Improper fractions are those that are greater than 1.	5. $\frac{3}{4}$ is the same as $\frac{6}{8}$.
6. Twelve is a multiple of 60.	7. Fifteen is a factor of 100.	8. These words are all spelled correctly: eighty, seventy, hunderd.	9. These are all prime numbers: 17, 23, 29.	10. These are all composite numbers: 21, 35, 71
11. 6.2356 is greater than 6.23567.	12. 0.7504 is less than 0.751.	13. 1239 is divisible by 3.	14. These are divisible by 5: 1500, 615, 230.	15. A 4-inch square has an area of 12 square inches.
16. The least common multiple of 3, 5, and 6 is 60.	17. The greatest common factor of 24, 48, and 72 is 6.	18. A 6-inch square has a perimeter of 24 inches.	19. $\frac{2}{3}$ is less than $\frac{3}{4}$.	20. 4,072 is divisible by 3.
21. $\frac{32}{48}$ can be reduced to $\frac{2}{3}$.	22. The average of 10, 20, and 24 is 15.	23. $\frac{10}{4}$ is the same as $2\frac{1}{4}$.	24. $\frac{2}{7}$ of 42 is 12.	25. 25% of 44 is 12.
26. $\frac{2}{3}$ of 30 is 20.	27. $\frac{5}{10}$ can be written as 0.05.	28. If y = 12, then 5y = 60.	29. $\frac{9}{10} - \frac{1}{5} = \frac{3}{10}$	30. A square is a special kind of quadrilateral.

Name ______________________ Date ______________

Telegrams

Your students have probably never received a telegram, but before the days of e-mail and fax machines, telegrams were used to send urgent messages. The Morse code, a system that uses dots and dashes to represent letters of the alphabet, was used to transmit telegrams over wires beginning in the mid-1800s. Telegrams were very expensive to send, and senders were charged fees based on the number of words and letters they transmitted. Consequently, telegrams were often very short and choppy and contained only essential words.

This is a game in which students will write crazy telegrams. First, ask 10 students to each call out a different letter of the alphabet. Write these 10 letters, in the order you receive them, on the chalkboard.

Instruct students to copy the 10 letters in the same order on a half sheet of paper, leaving a large space between letters. Then ask them to write a "telegram," filling out the ten spaces with words beginning with the letters printed on their paper. Some will make sense, and others will be completely ridiculous.

After allowing students a couple of minutes in which to compose their telegrams, ask each person to read his or her telegram aloud. If desired, give a small "prize" to the most ingenious outcome.

Example: The 10 letters chosen are: P Y F A M C B W E L.

Possible telegrams: Penny yearns for Amos. Must come before Weird Emil leaves.
Please yell for Amy. Marcella cares but won't ever learn.
Prompt your family. All may carry back white English lavender.

Variation: Ask the students to select 10 letters randomly to write on their pages, leaving a large space between letters. Then have each player pass the page to the student on the right (or left, etc.). In this way, each student will be writing a telegram using a different set of letters.

Name ______________________ Date ____________

Here's a fun oral game that requires absolutely no preparation, and the whole class can enjoy it at the same time!

To play this game, 1 student plays the part of a questioner, and all the other students must take turns answering her questions. It sounds simple enough, but there is always a letter that is taboo. First, the class must agree on a letter that is taboo, or forbidden. This letter must not be used in any of the answers, but the person who is asking the questions may use it if she likes. The questioner asks any questions she likes, hoping to catch as many players as possible using the forbidden letter. Players are required to answer questions as truthfully as possible.

Suppose that the class agrees that the letter **c** is the taboo letter for the first round. The questioner might ask the first player, "What is your favorite December holiday?" hoping that she will answer, "Christmas." But the clever player might instead answer, "New Year's Eve," or "the first day of winter."

Any player who uses the taboo letter gets a point. When the first questioner has asked every student a question for the first taboo letter, a new player becomes the questioner, and a new taboo letter is chosen. The winners are the players with the fewest number of points when time has expired.

Name ______________________ Date ____________

If you have just a few minutes of free class time, consider asking your students to answer one or more of these brainstorming questions. Here are some different ways in which the questions can be used:

- Quickly assign students to work in small groups and count together how many responses they can list in one minute. The team with the most oral answers wins the round. Play more rounds as time allows and have teams keep running totals for their scores.
- Work together as a class. Either record all responses yourself, or ask a student to do it. Post the lists around the room as a reminder of your brainstorming success. Refer to these lists in future classroom projects.

1. How many adjectives can you list that begin with the letter **H**?
2. How many fictional animal characters from children's literature can you name?
3. How many prime numbers can you list?
4. How many different punctuation marks can you list?
5. How many mountains (or mountain ranges) can you name?
6. How many Dr. Seuss titles can you remember?
7. A palindrome is a word that reads the same backwards and forwards. An example is *eve*. How many other palindromes can you list?
8. How many synonyms can you name for *big*?
9. How many African countries can you name?
10. How many verbs can you list that begin with **W**?
11. How many words can you list that rhyme with *bill*?
12. How many 4-syllable words can you list?
13. How many 10-letter words can you list?
14. How many occupations can you list that begin with **S**?

Name ______________________ Date ______________

Sound Off!

Here's a game that will get your students making a bit of noise, so be prepared! This is a quiz game, where teams will "ring" to answer questions. You can adapt the content of this game to cover material from your current units of study, or you may use the questions contained on the pages that follow.

Prepare for this game by photocopying the game boards on pages 127 and 128 onto transparencies. Write the names of the 6 categories for each round at the top of each column. Ideally you should make permanent overheads for the game boards, and add the categories with a wipe-off marker so that the game boards can be changed for future games. Or, if you are writing your own material, decide what categories of questions you will use, and prepare 5 questions for each category.

To play Sound Off!, first divide your class into 3 teams, and have the members of each team sit together. Instruct each team to appoint a scorekeeper to keep track of the team's points. This student may also try to "ring in" and answer questions. Give each team one of these names: Buzz, Honk, and Ding. Tell the students that when they wish to answer a question, they must call out the name of their team. You serve as judge and call on only the team you hear first.

Present the game board for the first round on the overhead projector. Read each category and a brief description of its contents, if necessary, as shown on pages 124–26. Decide which team goes first, and instruct 1 player on that team to choose the first question. The player might, for example, call out "Planets for 10 points." You then read aloud the corresponding question. Anyone who knows the answer can call out the name of her team. Select the student you heard first, and allow her a few seconds to give the answer. Students should not call out the answer; rather they should call out the name of their team.

If a student gives the correct answer, her team wins 10 points (or the number matching the clue). If the student misses the answer, her team loses that number of points. Cross off each question on the game board as it is used. If the first team answers incorrectly, the 2 remaining teams are allowed to "ring in." Again if a team answers correctly, they are awarded the points. If they are incorrect, they lose the points. If the second team also answers incorrectly, the third team may ring if they choose.

The winning team is the one with the most points after the class has played both Round 1 and Round 2.

Name ______________________ Date ______________

Notice that there are a few questions marked "POP." These are questions where all 3 teams can choose to double a portion of their earnings. When a student selects a question that is marked POP in your list, call out that word. Immediately each team should send 1 player to the chalkboard who writes a number on the board that represents the amount of points they are willing to wager. You then read the question, and every player at the chalkboard writes their answer. (There should be no talking allowed.)

Each team that is correct adds the wagered amount to their earnings. Each team that is incorrect must subtract that amount. For example, suppose that Honks have 50 points and they wish to wager 30 of it. Also suppose that the Dings have 80 points and they wish to wager 20 of it. If the Honk player writes the correct answer, the team's new score is 80 points. If the Ding's player answers incorrectly, that team's new score is 60 points.

Questions for Round 1:

Starts with "A"
10 points—This is the first of our 50 states alphabetically. (Alabama)
20 points—This word describes an athlete who plays for fun, not for pay. (amateur)
30 points—The structure of an organism is known as this "a" word. (anatomy)
40 points—A partner in crime is known as this. (accomplice)
50 points—This was a medieval form of chemistry in which scientists attempted to turn base metals into gold. (alchemy)

The U.S. Constitution
10 points—What is the name of the introduction to the Constitution? (Preamble)
20 points—According to the Constitution, how long does each U.S. senator serve? (6 years)
30 points—What is the name of the group of people who actually select the President? (electors)
40 points—What 3 qualifications of people seeking to be President are listed in Article 11 of the Constitution? (natural born citizen of the U.S., 35 years of age or older, resident of the U.S. for at least 14 years)
50 points—One amendment to the Constitution prohibited the manufacturing and selling of alcohol. Another amendment repealed that law. What amendments were these? (18th and 21st)

Name ______________________ Date ______________

The Calendar

10 points—How many months have exactly 30 days? (4: April, June, September, and November)

20 points—If Christmas falls on a Wednesday, then on what day will New Year's Eve land? (Tuesday)

30 points—When is Election Day? (The first Tuesday after the first Monday in November)

40 points—What is the date of the 50th day of the year? (Feb. 19)

50 points—For many years, the world followed a Julian calendar. In 1582, however, we switched to a different one that is still in use today. What is its name? (Gregorian, named after Pope Gregory who suggested that this calendar be used)

World Capitals (I will name the country; you name its capital.)

10 points—Italy (Rome)

20 points—Spain (Madrid)

POP!—Sweden (Stockholm)

40 points—Libya (Tripoli)

50 points—Nicaragua (Managua)

Planets

10 points—Which planet has the largest rings surrounding it? (Saturn)

20 points—Which planet is known as the "red" planet? (Mars)

30 points—Which planet has the largest diameter? (Jupiter)

POP!—Name all nine planets in our solar system in order, starting with the one closest to the sun. (Mercury, Venus, Earth, Mars, Jupiter, Saturn, Uranus, Neptune*, Pluto. * At certain times, Neptune and Plute trade places.)

50 points—The planet Mercury has the shortest revolution of all the planets. How long is one year on Mercury, as measured in Earth days? (88 days)

Words that Rhyme (I will supply clues; you name a pair of rhyming words that fit the clues.)

10 points—an extra seat (spare chair)

20 points—remorse over a handmade comforter (quilt guilt)

30 points—a female relative's bias (aunt's slant)

40 points—a doglike mammal's fishing equipment (jackal's tackle)

50 points—Escape artist's summer squash (Houdini's zucchini)

Questions for Round 2:

Ends with "Z"
20 points—This short exam is probably a word with which you are very familiar. (quiz)
40 points—A newly-opened can of soda will make this hissing sound. (fizz)
60 points—A form of American music (jazz)
80 points—This slang word means to tease or ridicule. (razz)
100 points—Something that is exciting or attractive is said to have this quality. (pizzazz)

Non-metric Measurements
20 points—How many teaspoons are in a tablespoon? (3)
40 points—How many cubic feet are in a cubic yard? (9)
POP!—How many pecks are in a bushel? (4)
80 points—How many cups are in gallon? (16)
100 points—How many furlongs are in a statute mile? (8)

State Nicknames (I will give a nickname; you tell the state to which it belongs.)
20 points—The Sooner State (Oklahoma)
40 points—The Empire State (New York)
60 points—The Keystone State (Pennsylvania)
80 points—The Magnolia State (Mississippi)
100 points—The Beehive State (Utah)

Presidential Nicknames (I will give a nickname; you tell the President to whom it was given.)
20 points—Ike (Dwight Eisenhower)
40 points—Jimmy (James Carter)
60 points—Tricky Dick (Richard Nixon)
80 points—The Great Communicator (Ronald Reagan)
100 points—Rough Rider (Theodore Roosevelt)

Chemical Elements and Symbols
20 points—What is the symbol for the element oxygen? (0)
40 points—What element is represented by the symbol N? (nitrogen)
POP!—The symbol Hg represents a poisonous metallic liquid. What is it? (mercury)
80 points—What are the symbols for gold and silver? (gold—Au, silver—Ag)
100 points—What state in the U.S. has an element named in its honor? (California; the element is californium)

Name ______________________ Date ______________

Game board for Round 1

10	10	10	10	10	10
20	20	20	20	20	20
30	30	30	30	30	30
40	40	40	40	40	40
50	50	50	50	50	50

Name ______________________ Date ______________

Game board for Round 2

20	20	20	20	20	20
40	40	40	40	40	40
60	60	60	60	60	60
80	80	80	80	80	80
100	100	100	100	100	100